Honey Feast

The text of this book was photoset
on a T x T II in 14 point Garamond, by
Mark Allen Donicht of Dharma Press,
Emeryville, California.
Design, calligraphy and illustrations
by Georgianna Greenwood.

ISBN 0-913668-27-3 paper
ISBN 0-913668-29-x cloth

Published by Apple Pie Press, Inc.
Distributed by
Ten Speed Press
Box 7123
Berkeley, Calif. 94707

Printed in The United States of America

Honey Feast

A SAMPLER OF HONEY RECIPES

APPLE PIE PRESS
TEN SPEED

Table of Contents

Quick Breads

Main dish Breads

Dressings

Introduction

Many people enjoy honey on toast or in their tea, but the taste of other honey foods has not encouraged them to explore further. This is regrettable, since honey is one of the few foods readily available pure and unadulterated—its natural chemistry keeps it fresh for years without additives or special care. A desire to enjoy honey more often should not be discouraged by the lack of interesting recipes. This book began as a search for foods that would appeal to the discriminating honey eater: someone who expects foods made with honey to meet the same standards as any other food he would choose to eat every day—they should be nutritious, varied, and appealing in taste, texture, and appearance.

Some early experiments were disappointing; conventional "healthfoods" offer a poor introduction to the scope of honey eating. They seem to be limited by an institutional approach, where the unilateral use of honey produces an array of foods that look and taste monotonously similar—soft, sweet, and brown, and generally unappetizing. Happily, this is not the inevitable result of using honey in baking. Honey goods do brown more, they are softer and moister than if made with sugar, and they enjoy a remarkable keeping quality. When these characteristics are put to deliberate use, rather than casually disregarded, they can make pastries of distinction.

Some guidelines to the use of honey come from ancient and traditional practices, since honey has been used in cooking at least since Roman times. It lends its perfume to delicate cheese mixtures; it enhances vegetables and occasionally meats; and it is the agent that causes cakes and cookies, over long periods of dark storage, to develop an incomparable bouquet of spices and fruits, each part distinguished in the whole beyond the limits of its single contribution. Honey cakes resembling spiced bread loaves continue to be baked in many European and Near East countries; flat cookies, usually called cakes, are carefully made and aged for months as part of holiday rituals. These specialities deserve attention from anyone who would know the pleasures of honey.

In small amounts, honey heightens flavor without itself being distinguishable—in greater proportion, it quickly tends to dominate a mixture. Light-colored honeys tend to have a less pronounced effect in flavor combinations, so they should be chosen when an unidentifiable sweetness is desired. Dark, mellow honeys such as buckwheat contribute flavor and are excellent in spicy pastries. Occasionally honeys such as eucalyptus are so strongly flavored that they are not recommended for general use—appreciate them on toast or in tea. A dish in which honey disguises or obliterates the natural flavors of the other ingredients is a disappointment even to a confirmed honey eater. Moderation in all things, but especially in honey!

Rigorous substitution of honey for sugar produces textural and taste differences that are not always desirable. Honey contains some vitamins and minerals while refined sugar does not, so one is inclined to use honey whenever culinary considerations do not weigh against it. People who choose for dietary reasons to exclude sugar entirely will become adept at making substitutions, not only within specific recipes but by developing new eating habits. Respect for good ingredients and good tastes is basic in any style of eating, and there are recipes in this collection to meet the requirements of many different individual diets.

In most mixtures honey can be substituted directly for sugar, allowing for its greater sweetening power and its additional flavoring effect: usually a smaller amount is wanted. The texture of puddings, custards, and pie fillings is virtually unaffected by this substitution. Honey provides nourishment for the growth of yeast in bread-baking and may improve the texture, as well as increasing keeping quality. In dense cakes honey is an apt ingredient; in high-rising layer cakes, complex adjustments are needed and there is little to recommend working these out: choose to make a more suitable pastry instead.

Freshly harvested honey is at its peak of flavor, so the fall of the year is a perfect time to purchase and sample different varieties of honey to compare their highly individual flavors. Honey tasting should be done in very close succession to appreciate differences between kinds; they are more distinct than you might anticipate. Choose a selection with a range of qualities: dark, light, strong; try honey in the comb as well as liquid. Thyme honey from Mt. Hymettus in Greece, available in many Mediterranean markets, is distinctive as a contrast to domestic kinds. Orange blossom honey from California is ranked among the world's great flavors, as are Scottish heather honey, wild thyme honey from Provence, rosemary honey from Spain. If you have any difficulty in finding honey at local markets, you can often find an interesting selection in healthfood stores and gourmet specialty shops.

Our experiments with honey culminated in a Honey Feast in July, 1973; some fifteen friends assembled for a meal composed almost entirely of honey dishes. This meal posed a central question: would the repeated use of honey, course after course, so dull the palate that all flavors merged into a dreadful sameness? By the time the group had reached dessert and waited with an attitude of pleased expectation, we had our answer. The total effect was pleasing. Honey had been put to such diverse use, here blending into a dish, there offset with lemon, that it did not overwhelm. The menu itself was not a model of composition, but the meal was an interesting demonstration of the range of taste experience offered by cooking with honey. Highlights were tomato sherbet, where honey vanishes into a mixture with incomparable freshness of flavor; and homemade honey ice cream, balanced with orange peel and crunchy with toasted almonds. Platters of pastries included many-layered baklava, spice cookies shaped like fat mushrooms, slices of poppyseed strudel with its coil of dark filling, golden Greek cookies rolled in walnuts, squares of Russian nut candy. A dish of fresh summer plums in many colors, drizzled with honey and garlanded with mounds of sour cream, was passed. Lots of strong coffee. We enjoyed rich colors, contrasting textures, and variety of flavor. Collected here are many more recipes that lead to further appreciation of honey; like the meal, the book is a sampler of the many tastes of honey.

Honey Feast
29 JULY 1973

Tomato sherbet in avocado cups
Beet aspic
Summer plum salad
garden cucumbers
pickled beets
yogurt
pita
Lamb tajine
Moroccan tajine qamama
tzimmes
carrots in Pomegranate sauce
steamed
couscous

sorbet aux cerises Drouant
glace au miel

Finikia
mohnstrudel
Sweetmeats au miel

Guide to Using the Recipes

Read each recipe from start to finish before you begin. Make appropriate allowances of time needed to prepare ingredients–chopping nuts, grating carrots, preparing syrup or glaze. Many traditional European recipes call for chilling dough overnight before rolling and baking, and many honey cakes and cookies must be baked well in advance and wrapped and stored to develop flavor before they are eaten.

Choose only the freshest ingredients available.

Prepare your own candied fruit peels for unsurpassed flavor. Many European pastries include fruit peels, freshly grated or candied, as a contrast to the flavors of honey and spices; packaged peels invariably lack flavor and taste of preservatives. Your own peels will be pure and intensely flavorful. Candy the fruits at some convenient time and store them, tightly covered, until needed.

Grind your own spices whenever possible. Always grate nutmeg freshly. Cardamon is easily pounded in a mortar and pestle; remove the small aromatic seeds from their pale husks and grind finely. Cinnamon, mace, cloves, and ginger are acceptable in packaged form, but they lose flavor once jars are opened; check for fragrance and replace them when they have lost potency. Whole spices may be ground in a small electric coffee-and-spice grinder. Reduce quantities suggested in recipes to compensate for the enhanced intensity of flavor.

Always grate fresh orange rind and fresh lemon rind when called for in a recipe. Choose another dish rather than substitute bottled rinds. Grating directly into the mixing bowl prevents loss of the aromatic oils that spray from the scraped skin; estimate that a medium orange yields 2 teaspoons grated rind and a lemon yields 1 teaspoon.

Honey combines best with other ingredients when it is slightly warmed to reduce viscosity. The measuring cup can be oiled for ease in pouring honey out. If honey should crystallize in the jar, it is readily liquefied by placing the open container in a pan of hot water or a 200° oven until smooth again.

Have all ingredients at room temperature unless otherwise indicated. Butter combines best at room temperature, except in pastry where you want to keep it from merging with the flour. Egg whites whip to best volume at room temperature or a little warmer (the top of an oven, perhaps). Cold eggs or milk added to a mixture can slow down combination processes in baking and lead to inferior texture.

Prepare baking pans as indicated in recipe. To dust a greased pan with flour, put a tablespoonful of flour in the pan, tilt so the surface is coated, turn pan over and tap out any excess. Butter tends to scorch at higher oven temperatures, so vegetable oil or shortening is preferable. Oil can be applied efficiently with a pastry brush; it is evenly distributed and coats every corner.

Cool baked good as directed. This final step is essential for good texture in the finished product and for ease in removing from the baking pans.

A description of recommended equipment follows the recipe section.

Ingredients

Flour ∼ Unbleached white flour. Sift before measuring for pastries; sifting is not required for breads. To measure, fill cup without shaking or packing and level with a straight-edged knife or dough scraper. ¾ cup whole wheat flour may be substituted for each cup of white flour.

Butter ᙂ Butter usually gives best flavor, but for economy or convenience any solid shortening may be substituted—margarine, hydrogenated shortening, or lard—in equal amounts.

Honey ᙂ Our recipes call for liquid honey only. Use whatever flavor you enjoy for spreading on bread and toast, but for baking avoid the strong-flavored varieties such as eucalyptus. Dark honeys are excellent in spiced cakes and cookies; lightly colored honeys are appropriate when a less noticeable flavor is wanted. To get the full amount of honey measured, use a rubber spatula to scrape the cup; oiling the cup before measuring the honey also makes it easier to empty. If honey crystallizes, set the jar in a pan of hot, not boiling, water until it is smooth again.

Eggs ᙂ Large eggs

Yeast ᙂ Active dry yeast is used in all our bread recipes. Store packaged dry yeast on a cool shelf and use before the date stamped on the package. Bulk dry yeast should be stored, covered, in the refrigerator; 1 Tbsp. = 1 pkg. yeast. Dissolve in 110° water. Cake yeast is more perishable. Keep it refrigerated and use it soon after purchase. Crumble into 85° water. Use a candy thermometer to measure water temperature.

TABLE *of* EQUIVALENTS

1 pound honey	. . .	1⅓ cups
¼ pound butter	. . .	½ cup (one stick)
5 large eggs	. . .	1 cup
1 pound flour	. . .	4 cups
1 pound sugar	. . .	2 cups
½ pound nuts	. . .	2 cups
1 lemon	. . .	about 2 Tbsp. juice
1 lemon	. . .	about 1 tsp. grated rind
1 orange	. . .	about ½ cup juice
1 orange	. . .	about 2 tsp. grated rind
1 pkg. gelatine	. . .	1 Tbsp.
1 pkg. active dry yeast	. . .	1 Tbsp.
1 cup	. . .	16 Tablespoons, 8 ounces
3 teaspoons	. . .	1 Tablespoon
2 Tablespoons	. . .	1 ounce

Breads

Bread and honey, the fabled monarch's treat, really involves two considerations: there is bread eaten with honey, and there is bread made with honey. Best eaten with honey, we think, are nutty wholegrain loaves—not soft white bread presumably fit for a queen. Bread made with oatmeal, whole wheat, graham, and other coarse flours have a firm texture and robust flavor, as well as added food value. Honey, if used in these breads, is an incidental flavor; but it is unexcelled as a spread for generous slices of fresh bread or hot muffins. Then there are breads made with honey, the antecedents of all cakes and pastries. Honey-sweetened breads have been known from Biblical times, and honey cakes are still made today, refined and individual as they have passed from generation to generation as a traditional food of different cultures.

Homemade bread is easy to make once you master a few unsophisticated techniques, and no other cooking process offers such tactile enjoyment as kneading and shaping a vigorous, responsive yeast dough. Breads that you make cost less, stay fresh longer than commercial loaves without additives; they contain only what you choose, and by selecting fresh, healthful ingredients you can produce flavorful, nourishing breads. The food value of bread can be increased by adding soy flour, dry milk powder, and wheat germ; protein and vitamins are added, and flavor and texture are often improved. Whenever a recipe calls for 8 cups of flour, use 7 cups regular unbleached flour plus ½ cup soy flour, ¼ cup dry milk, and ¼ cup wheat germ. This formula is derived from experiments at Cornell University where it was found that bread thus enriched would sustain life. The formula is simple enough to remember and incorporate into everyday cooking practices.

The first step in yeast bread is to combine the dry yeast in warm water with sugar or honey and set in a warm spot to start the growth process; this mixture actively bubbles in a short time if the yeast is vigorous. Thus stimulated it combines more effectively with the flours and flavoring ingredients in the next step of mixing. Yeast, flour, and temperature all affect the rising time of a particular batch of bread; once it has been kneaded and put to rise in a warm place, the bread sets its own pace. Judge not by the clock but by observation and testing when bread is ready for punching down or shaping. Dough should double in bulk the first time and very nearly double the second, although it grows more quickly this time. To verify, push your fingers into the dough—if it immediately expands into the depressions, it has not reached full growth; a clear dent remains when it is ready for the next process. As long as this sequence is observed, you can bake bread in any size or shape you like. Bread underrisen is heavy and yeasty; overrisen it is porous and dry. Yeast breads need to cool before slicing or they collapse; remove from pans and set on a rack to cool evenly in order to get best texture.

European bakers for centuries have created elaborate breads for festival occasions, flavored with spices and fruits, taking traditional shapes and decorations that signify Christmas or Easter. Towering braids decorate Russian feast tables, Hungarians bend poppyseed strudel into a horseshoe for Christmas, tall Italian paentone are studded with candied fruit and nuts, Greek and Yugoslavian breads are given shiny mahogany honey glazes. Many of these breads are based on a supple, egg-rich sweet dough, easily shaped and complemented by a variety of fillings. Ohrenjaca, a Slavic holiday bread, is filled with walnuts, honey, and fruit rinds, set off by a spoon of whiskey, an elusive and delicious combination. Poppyseed fillings are treasured in many Balkan cultures, the seeds ground at the last moment for fresh flavor, honey, nuts, and raisins added; while the subtle, almost dry quality is not pleasing to everyone, it is to many people a requisite flavor of Christmas.

Honey is the ideal companion for many quick breads eaten hot from the oven. Muffins, pancakes, flaky biscuits, flamboyant squash cornbread—these are perfect rushed to the table where soft butter and honey are ready for them. A Mexican bread, *sopaipillas,* is fried, the little squares puffing into hollow pillows to be torn open at a corner, honey and butter stuffed inside. Moroccan orange doughnuts are fried and dipped into warm honey syrup, making one of those extraordinary Middle Eastern confections. Bran coffeecake and nut crumbcake, served warm, need no additional topping—their measure of honey is baked in.

Some quick breads, where baking powder and soda are used as leavening agents, benefit from aging overnight; flavors smooth out and texture improves. This is particularly true of honey breads; flavors merge and develop in leisurely fashion, and the breads stay fresh and moist for days. Honey gives character to walnut bread, orange bread, and a plain, unexpected Kentucky bread made with graham flour. Here using dark honeys will give more pronounced flavor, light honeys may seem sweeter. In the breads with fruit and spices, honey blends into a distinctive combination flavor.

Pancakes and waffles are invaluable in any cook's repertoire because they make a delicious meal with little effort or expense. When they are good, they are outstanding—hot, fragrant, and satisfying. Like pudding, hot cakes require a sauce—and the variety of possible toppings makes these dishes infinitely adaptable. Honey is well chosen for the bit of sweetening that goes into a batter, but it is unexcelled as a topping—plain, in honey butter, in creamy syrups. Sour cream or yogurt can be mixed with a little honey as a side dressing.

Cereals enriched by fruits, nuts, and honey and served with milk also make a meal. Muesli, the Swiss combination developed years ago as a healthful breakfast, is based on grains and shredded raw fruit. Granola, the cereal sensation of recent years, is also based on mixed grains that are sweetened and toasted with nuts and kernels. Both combinations are simple formulas meant to be varied according to ingredients at hand; it is most rewarding to develop your personal combination.

STEEL-CUT OATMEAL BREAD

Nuggets of coarsely cut oatmeal give this bread a fine chewy texture. It makes superlative toast, and any short ends may be cut into squares and fried to make soup croutons.

¼ cup honey or molasses	1 Tbsp. active dry yeast
2 Tbsp. butter	1 tsp. sugar or honey
1 Tbsp. salt	¼ tsp. ginger
2 cups steel-cut oatmeal	½ cup warm water (110°)
2 cups boiling water	5-6 cups flour

Place honey, butter, salt, and oatmeal in a large mixing bowl or the bowl of a heavy-duty mixer; pour 2 cups boiling water over them. Stir well and cool to lukewarm. Shortly before it is ready, dissolve yeast in ½ cup water with sugar and ginger in a ceramic bowl and set in a warm, draft-free place until it bubbles actively. Stir or beat 1 cup flour into the cooled porridge, add yeast mixture, then additional flour up to a total of 6 cups, using only enough to make an easily handled dough. Turn out of the bowl onto a floured board and let rest 10 minutes. Then knead until smooth and elastic. Make a neat ball and place in a greased bowl, cover with a damp towel, and let rise until double (1–2 hours). Butter two 9x5 loaf pans. Punch down dough and divide in two parts, shaping into loaves to fit pans. Let rise until double, about one hour. Preheat oven to 400°. Bake 30–40 minutes, until browned and hollow-sounding when thumped. Remove from pans at once and cool on racks.

AUNT VAN'S OATMEAL BREAD

1 ¾ cups boiling water
1 cup rolled oats
3 tsp. salt
1 Tbsp. butter
¼ cup molasses
¼ cup honey

½ cup warm water (110°)
2 Tbsp. active dry yeast
1 tsp. sugar or honey
¼ tsp. ginger
5 ½ cups flour

Pour boiling water over the oats in a bowl; add the salt, butter, molasses, and honey, and let the mixture sit for one hour. Shortly before the hour is up, combine the yeast, ½ cup warm water, sugar, and ginger in a small bowl and set in a warm, draft-free place until it bubbles actively. Combine the yeast with 5 cups flour. Then add the oatmeal mixture and stir well to make a stiff dough. Turn out onto a board covered with the remaining ½ cup flour and knead well, until the dough is smooth, shiny, and elastic. Form into a ball and place in a greased bowl, turning once to grease the top. Cover and let rise in a warm place until doubled, about one hour. Preheat oven to 375°. Butter two 8x4 loaf pans. Punch dough down with a single blow of the fist. Knead briefly. Divide in half and form into loaves. Place in pans, let rise until double, and bake for 40 minutes, until nicely browned and hollow-sounding when thumped. Turn out onto cooling racks. Serve for breakfast with butter and honey, or with soup for lunch.

The Cheese Board's EGG & HONEY BREAD

Delicious fresh breads are made daily at The Cheese Board, a tiny shop in Berkeley crammed with best quality cheeses in astonishing variety. Their Egg and Honey bread is also featured at the Swallow cafe in the University of California Art Museum, where all sandwiches begin with homemade bread and the balance of the menu is prepared with equal care.

1 Tbsp. active dry yeast	2 eggs
1 tsp. sugar	3 Tbsp. butter
1 cup warm water (110°)	1 cup milk
4-5 Tbsp. honey	6-8 cups flour
1 Tbsp. salt	

Dissolve the yeast and sugar in warm water in a medium ceramic bowl and set in a warm, draft-free place until it bubbles vigorously. Heat the milk to boiling in a small saucepan. In a large mixing bowl or the bowl of a heavy-duty mixer place the honey, salt, eggs, and butter, and pour the hot milk over them. Stir to combine and cool to lukewarm. Add 1 cup flour and then add the yeast mixture. Add flour a few cups at a time, mixing thoroughly, until you have a smooth dough that clears the sides of the bowl. Turn out onto a lightly floured surface and knead until shiny and elastic. Form into a ball and place in a greased bowl, cover and set in a warm place to rise until double. Punch down with a single blow of your fist and divide into four parts. Shape into neat firm balls of dough, pulling the ends together and sealing well, and place in greased small foil pie pans. Place them on a baking sheet, well separated, for ease in handling. Set to rise again, covered, until double. Preheat oven to 350°. Bake loaves 30–40 minutes, until rich golden brown and hollow-sounding when thumped. Remove from pans and cool on racks. As you might expect, this bread will make a fantastic toasted cheese sandwich—the tang of sharp cheddar is effectively set off by the slightly sweet bread.

HONEY RYE BREAD

1½ cups milk	2 Tbsp. active dry yeast
¼ cup honey	1 tsp. sugar or honey
4 tsp. salt	¼ tsp. ginger
2 Tbsp. bland oil	3 cups rye flour
1 Tbsp. caraway, fennel, or anise seeds, *optional*	3½ cups flour
	melted butter, for brushing
1 cup warm water (110°)	on loaves

Place the honey, salt, oil, and seeds in a large bowl or the bowl of a heavy-duty mixer. Heat the milk to boiling and pour it over them; cool to lukewarm. In a small ceramic bowl combine the yeast, water, sugar, and ginger; set in a warm, draft-free place until it bubbles vigorously. Mix one cup flour into the cooled liquids; add the yeast mixture and combine thoroughly. Add the rye flour and white flour a cup at a time, mixing well. Use enough flour to make a stiff dough. Turn out onto a floured board and let rest for 10 minutes. Then knead until smooth and elastic. Form into a neat ball and place in a large greased bowl, turning once to grease the top. Cover and set in a warm place to rise until doubled (45 minutes to an hour). Butter two 9x5 loaf pans. Turn the dough out onto a floured board and divide in two. Shape into loaves, place in pans, cover and let rise until doubled again. Preheat oven to 375°. Bake 50 minutes or until browned and hollow-sounding when thumped. Remove from pans and cool on racks. While warm, brush the tops with melted butter.

SUBSTANTIAL GRAHAM BREAD

Firm and delicious, this is my favorite all-purpose bread.

¼ cup butter	1 Tbsp. active dry yeast
3 Tbsp. honey	1 tsp. sugar or honey
1 Tbsp. salt	¼ tsp. ginger
1 large can evaporated milk	½ cup warm water (110°)
	3 cups graham flour
1 additional can hot water	5-6 cups white flour*

Place the butter, honey, salt, and evaporated milk in a large bowl or the bowl of a heavy-duty mixer. Pour hot water over, mix, and cool to lukewarm. Shortly before it is ready, place the yeast, 1 tsp. sugar, ginger, and warm water in a small ceramic bowl and set in a warm, draft-free place until it bubbles vigorously. Mix into the cooled liquids 1 cup white flour; add the yeast mixture, then the graham flour, and additional white flour as needed to make an elastic and shiny dough that readily leaves the sides of the bowl. Turn out on a floured board and knead until uniformly smooth and elastic. Place in a large, greased ceramic bowl, cover, and set in a warm place to double in bulk. Grease four 8x4 loaf pans. When dough has doubled, punch down with a single blow of your fist. Work dough together again and divide into four parts. Roll each portion with a rolling pin into a rectangle about 8x12″ and roll up very tightly, as for a jelly roll, from the narrower side. Pinch the long seam together securely, turn this to the bottom, and tuck the ends under smoothly, pinching into place. This is the technique for making shapely loaves. Place in prepared pans and let rise until half again as large; this should be a firm-textured loaf, so should not rise until light. Preheat oven to 375°. Bake about one hour, until well browned and hollow-sounding when thumped. Remove from pans at once and cool on racks. Simply wonderful with butter and honey.

* If desired, substitute for one cup of white flour the following: ¼ cup wheat germ, ¼ cup dried milk powder, and ½ cup soy flour. This addition, based on the Cornell University enrichment formula, adds protein with no loss in texture or flavor.

RAISIN HEALTH BREAD

Inspired by a recipe in the monthly Pacific Gas and Electric Newsletter, this bread is full of good things. To conserve our energy resources, double this recipe and bake four loaves while you're at it.

⅓ cup seedless raisins	2⅓ cups whole wheat flour
⅓ cup golden raisins	1 cup flour
1 Tbsp. active dry yeast	3 Tbsp. raw wheat germ
1 tsp. sugar or honey	⅓ cup powdered milk
⅛ tsp. ginger	1½ tsp. salt
1⅓ cups warm water (110°)	¼ cup hulled sunflower seeds
2½ Tbsp. bland oil	
¼ cup honey	1 egg yolk mixed with 1 tsp. water, for glaze
1 egg	
½ cup cracked wheat	

Place the raisins in a bowl, cover with hot water, and let stand until cool. Drain, then dry them on paper towels; set aside. In a small ceramic bowl combine the yeast, ⅓ cup of warm water, sugar, and ginger; place in a warm, draft-free place until it bubbles vigorously. In a small bowl combine the oil, honey, and egg, mixing well; stir in the cracked wheat and let stand. In a large bowl or the bowl of a heavy-duty mixer combine the flours, dry milk powder, and salt. Add the yeast mixture, then the honey-egg mixture, then the remaining 1 cup warm water. Mix well to combine all ingredients. Finally stir in the raisins and sunflower seeds. Turn the dough out on a floured surface and knead until the dough is smooth, shiny, and elastic, adding flour if needed. Form into a neat ball, place in a large greased bowl, turning once to grease the top; cover, and set in a warm place to rise until doubled in bulk (about two hours). Butter heavily two 8x4 loaf pans. Punch down with a single blow of your fist and divide into two parts. Shape each into a loaf and place in prepared pans. Cover and let rise until doubled, about one hour. Preheat oven to 375°. Brush the tops with the egg yolk and water mixed together. Bake 35-40 minutes, until well browned and hollow-sounding when thumped. Turn out onto racks to cool.

ENGLISH MUFFINS

Like city kids who think that milk comes in cardboard cartons and know nothing of cows, many people think that English muffins are something one only buys. If you make your own, people will be terribly impressed. This recipe uses whole wheat flour and currants for extra taste and nutrition, but you can easily make the plain familiar style. Good form requires that you split muffins with a fork, making the maximum number of craters for the butter to melt into.

2 Tbsp. honey	1 tsp. sugar or honey
1 tsp. salt	1 cup warm water (110°)
3 Tbsp. butter	4 cups flour
½ cup currants	1½ cups whole wheat flour
1 cup milk	cornmeal, for shaping
1 Tbsp. active dry yeast	

Scald the milk in a small heavy saucepan. Stir in the honey, salt, butter, and currants and cool to lukewarm. In a small ceramic bowl combine the yeast, water, and sugar and set in a warm, draft-free place until bubbling vigorously. In a large bowl or the bowl of a heavy-duty mixer measure 1½ cups whole wheat flour and 1½ cups white flour; add the yeast mixture and combine thoroughly. Add the milk mixture and beat until smooth. Stir in remaining 2½ cups of flour to make a stiff dough. Turn out on a floured board and knead briefly until it forms a manageable ball; some stickiness is all right. Place the ball in a greased bowl, turning once to grease the top; cover and let rise in a warm place until doubled, about one hour. Punch down and divide in half. Grease a baking sheet. Cover a pastry board with a thick layer of cornmeal; on it pat each half of the dough into a ½" thick rectangle. Then cut into circles using a floured 3"– 4" cutter. Place the muffins two inches apart on the baking sheet, cover, and let rise until doubled, about 45 minutes. Ideally English muffins are baked on a griddle; if unavailable, use a heavy frying pan that heats evenly. Heat the surface until medium hot and butter lightly. Place muffins on it, cornmeal side down, and bake 10 minutes to a side, or until well browned. Cool on wire racks. Split and toast; serve with lots of butter and honey.

BASIC RICH COFFEECAKE DOUGH

Supple and easily shaped, this basic dough lends itself to a variety of fillings, and the large quantity can be used to make a number of different breads. All ingredients can be reduced by one half to make a smaller quantity, two standard loaves. Baking the plain dough in loaves or buns gives a brioche-like bread, moist and good for toasting.

1 cup butter	1 tsp. ginger
¾ cup sugar	1 cup warm water (110°)
2 tsp. salt	grated rind of one lemon
1½ cups hot milk	6 whole eggs
4 Tbsp. active dry yeast	6 egg yolks
4 tsp. sugar	8-10 cups flour

Place the butter, sugar, and salt in a large mixing bowl or the bowl of a heavy-duty mixer. Pour the hot milk over it and let cool to lukewarm. Meanwhile mix together the yeast, sugar, ginger, and warm water in a small ceramic bowl and place in a warm draft-free place until it bubbles vigorously. To the milk mixture, add eggs and egg yolks and beat well. Grate the lemon directly into the bowl so no aromatic oils are lost. Add 1 cup flour, mixing well; add the yeast. Continue adding flour until you have a smooth, medium-soft dough that is shiny and elastic. Knead until it cleans the sides of the bowl. Cover with a towel and place in a warm place to rise, about 1½ hours. When poking with your fingers leaves clear impressions about 1″ deep, it is ready to punch down. Divide into the desired portions. This amount makes four 9x5 loaves or equivalent shapes. Use any fillings. Let rise again until doubled, 30–45 minutes. Bake according to recipe directions, usually 350° for 45 minutes to one hour. Coffeecakes made with this dough stay fresh for a couple of days or freeze beautifully.

STICKY BUNS

Honey is wonderful as the basis for sticky buns; simply butter a baking pan lavishly (about 2 tablespoonfuls) and put ¼″ of honey in the bottom. Prepare rolls in any shape desired, place in pan, let rise, bake; allow to cool a few minutes before inverting the pan. The glaze is very glossy and delicious.

One fourth recipe Basic Coffeecake Dough	¼ cup candied lemon peel, homemade preferred
melted butter	2 Tbsp. honey
cinnamon	¼ cup chopped blanched almonds
½ cup chopped prunes	

Roll the dough into a rectangle about 9x12″. Spread with melted butter and sprinkle heavily with cinnamon. Combine the prunes, lemon peel, honey, and nuts and spread evenly over the dough. Roll up the dough, cut it into nine pieces about 1″ thick, and place them cut side down in the honey-lined pan. Let rise until double. Preheat oven to 375°. Bake 25 minutes, or until browned and firm. Let cool in pan a few minutes, then turn out to complete cooling.

LITHUANIAN POPPYSEED LOAF
Kaledu pyragas

One half recipe Basic Coffeecake Dough
½ cup poppyseeds
2 cups golden raisins
¼ cup honey (as needed), warmed

Knead the poppyseeds and raisins into the coffeecake dough after it is punched down. Or, if you are preparing only half the amount of dough, incorporate them after the eggs are added in the original mixing. If raisins appear dry, refresh them by immersing in hot water 15 minutes and draining well. Shape into two loaves and place in buttered 9x5 loaf pans. Let rise until doubled, about 1½ hours. Bake at 350° about one hour; reduce heat to 325° if they are browning too rapidly. Five minutes before done, remove the bread from the oven and brush with the warmed honey. Sprinkle additional poppyseeds on top, if desired. After five minutes additional baking, the glaze will be rich brown. Despite its high gloss, it is not sticky. Remove from pans and cool on a rack.

PUTICA

This Yugoslavian pastry with an unconventional, rather dry chocolate filling appears on holiday tables.

One half recipe Basic Coffeecake Dough
½ pound chopped walnuts (about 1½ cups)
¼ pound chopped raisins

4 oz. bitter chocolate, grated*
½ cup honey
cream
milk. for glaze

Mix together the filling ingredients, adding enough cream to make a smooth paste. Divide the coffeecake dough into two parts and roll into rectangles about ½" thick. Spread with the filling. Roll up as for a jelly roll and place in greased 9x5 loaf pans; if preferred, shape into 12" rolls and place well apart on a greased baking sheet. Let rise until double. Bake at 350° 25–30 minutes, until well browned. Brush top with milk as soon as the pastries come from the oven. Remove to racks to cool. Serve plain or with butter.

* Use a hand-held Mouli grater or counter-top Swedish nut grinder to grate chocolate; otherwise the chocolate melts in your hand as you hold it against a box grater.

OHRENJACA

Rich and satisfying, this Czechoslovakian nut-filled pastry has a special ingredient: whiskey. The flavor blends into the filling for an elusive and remarkable effect.

Three quarters recipe Basic Coffeecake Dough	grated rind of one orange
	grated rind of one lemon
1 pound chopped walnuts	1 Tbsp. whiskey
1 cup milk	1 cup honey

Scald the milk and pour it over the walnuts. Grate the fruit peels into the mixture, stir in the whiskey and honey until smooth. Let cool. Divide the coffeecake dough into three parts and roll each into a rectangle ¼" thick. Spread with the nut filling, leaving one inch at the far end for ease in sealing. Roll tightly as for a jelly roll, lengthwise, making rolls about 12" long. Place well apart on a large greased baking sheet or two, or shape into loaves and bake in three 9x5 pans. Let rise until double and bake at 350° about 45 minutes, until browned and firm. Remove to cooling racks and let cool before slicing.

ORANGE HONEY COFFEECAKE

One half recipe Basic
  Coffeecake Dough
½ cup butter, at room
  temperature
½ cup honey
grated rind of one orange

½ cup candied orange
  peel, chopped, home-
  made preferred
¾ cup walnuts, finely
  chopped or grated

Glaze: 1 egg yolk, 2 Tbsp. cream

Combine the soft butter, honey, and the grated rind of one orange. Cream together with the tips of your fingers or with a hand mixer. Roll out the dough into a large rectangle ½" thick. Spread thinly with the filling and sprinkle with candied orange peel and walnuts. Roll up tightly as for a jelly roll. With a rolling pin, flatten this to an inch in thickness. Cut into three long strips and cut these lengthwise to make six strips. Join the ends of three strips together and braid. Place in a buttered 9x5 loaf pan. Repeat to make two loaves. Let rise until light. Brush with a glaze made by mixing together an egg yolk and 2 Tbsp. cream. Bake at 350° about one hour; reduce heat to 325° if browning too rapidly. Remove from the pans as soon as the loaves come from the oven; cool on racks. Should any leftover slices dry out, spread with a little butter on both sides and brown lightly in a skillet. This process seems to refresh the flavor and texture of many slightly stale baked goods.

HONEY ALMOND TWIST

One fourth recipe
   Basic Coffeecake Dough
¼ cup honey
¼ cup sugar

¼ cup butter
¼ cup flour
½ cup sliced unblanched
   almonds

Butter a 10″ round baking pan; it can be a spring form pan or a skillet. Shape the dough into a long rope less than one inch in diameter, rolling between the hands and against a bread board. Place this in the pan, starting at the outer edge and twisting continually as you coil toward the center. Cover and let rise until double. When the dough has risen sufficiently so that the pan surface is completely covered, mix the topping ingredients together and spread gently over the cake, avoiding the outer edge (which burns too quickly). Preheat oven to 375°. Bake about 30 minutes, until golden. Remove from pan after five minutes and cool on rack.

HUNGARIAN CHRISTMAS STRUDEL

Christmas strudels, traditional in Balkan countries, are not made from the near-transparent stretched strudel dough but use a dense, somewhat flaky butter dough. Walnut or prune fillings may be used, as well as the poppyseed. Christmas morning breakfast in our house always included walnut strudel piled with paper-thin slices of ham, a once-a-year special sandwich.

1 oz. fresh yeast
   (cake type)
¾ cup warm water (85°)
1 Tbsp. sugar

3½ cups flour + 1 Tbsp.
½ tsp. salt
1 cup butter
3 egg yolks

Preheat oven to 350°. Lightly grease a large rectangular baking sheet or jelly roll pan. Soak the yeast with the sugar in warm water in a small ceramic bowl; it need not appear to bubble. Place the flour in a large mixing bowl, sprinkle the salt over it, and cut in the butter as for pie crust with a pastry blender until the mixture resembles coarse meal. Make a well in the center and add the egg yolks and yeast mixture. Toss together gently with a fork and then with your fingertips until the flour is well coated by the liquids and the dough forms a soft ball. Divide in three parts and roll each one out on a lightly floured board to a 12x12 rectangle. Spread with poppyseed filling, leaving ½" at the far end uncovered for easy sealing. Roll up tightly as for jelly roll and place the cylinders side by side, two inches apart, on the baking sheet. Let rise 15 minutes. Bake 45 minutes, until well browned and firm to a touch. Cool thoroughly on racks. Slice ⅜" thick to serve. Tightly wrapped, this keeps for days or weeks.

Poppyseed Filling

    8 ounces poppyseeds
    ½ cup butter
    ½ cup honey
    2 Tbsp. cream
    1 cup chopped walnuts
    ½ cup golden raisins

The night before, cover the poppyseeds with boiling water and let stand. Next day, drain well and grind. Special German poppyseed grinders are available at speciality shops, or use the fine blade of a meat grinder and put seeds through several times. Cream the butter with the honey till light; add cream, then ground poppyseeds. Stir in nuts and raisins. Use to fill Christmas strudel or *Hamentaschen*.

ETHIOPIAN HONEY BREAD

Coriander is perhaps the oldest spice known to man. The seeds of coriander have been found in Egyptian tombs, and Old Testament references to this spice show that it was well known to early Jews. A native of the Mediterranean area, it now grows throughout the world. It was the favored spice of American colonial cookie bakers, but few modern Americans can identify the flavor. This Ethiopian honey bread is a strong argument for keeping a jar of ground coriander on the shelf; its lively flavor and fragrance are readily appreciated.

1 Tbsp. active dry yeast	½ tsp. cinnamon
¼ cup warm water (110°)	¼ tsp. ground cloves
1 tsp. sugar or honey	1½ tsp. salt
⅛ tsp. ginger	1 cup warm milk
1 egg	4 Tbsp. sweet butter,
½ cup honey	melted and cooled
1 Tbsp. ground coriander	4½ cups flour

Combine the yeast, water, sugar, and ginger in a small ceramic bowl and set in a warm, draft-free place until it bubbles vigorously. Combine the egg, honey, spices, and salt in a large mixing bowl or the bowl of a heavy-duty mixer. Add the milk and 4 Tbsp. melted butter; mix in 1 cup flour. Add the yeast mixture and beat until all ingredients are well blended. Add flour ½ cup at a time, using only enough to make a soft dough. Use your hands if needed to work in the last flour. Turn out on a lightly floured surface and knead the bread by folding it end to end, pressing down and pushing forward several times with the heel of your hand. The dough will be sticky; use a dough scraper to clear the board and turn the mass of dough; avoid adding more flour. In about five minutes the dough will become smoother and more elastic.

Shape into a rough ball and place in a large bowl, covered, to rise until double in bulk. Butter heavily a 3-quart round baking dish 3″ deep, such as a casserole or enamelled dutch oven. Punch down the dough with a single blow of your fist. Knead for a few minutes, shape into a rough ball, and place in the prepared pan. Press it down so the bottom is covered completely. Cover and let rise until doubled again, reaching the top of the pan. Preheat oven to 300°. Bake 50–60 minutes, until nicely rounded on top and light golden brown. Leave in pan 5 minutes, then turn out and cool on a rack. This bread is delicious plain, but it is traditionally spread with butter and honey. Keeps exceedingly well.

WALNUT HONEY BREAD

Teatime is a ritual generally neglected in American eating practice, but it seems a very good alternative to lunch on long working days when supper will be late. Convention specifies a selection of three, one of them savory, a sweet, and a fresh bread. This walnut loaf is virtually classic as a tea bread, served with butter and honey.

1 cup milk	2½ cups flour
1 cup honey	1 tsp. salt
¼ cup sugar	1 tsp. baking soda
¼ cup butter	½ cup walnuts, broken
2 egg yolks	

Preheat oven to 325°. Butter and flour a 9x5 loaf pan. In a large saucepan heat the milk and add honey and sugar, stirring until the sugar is melted and homogeneous. Cool. Mix in the butter and egg yolks. Sift together the flour, salt, and soda; mix in thoroughly. Stir in walnuts. Pour into the pan and let stand 20 minutes. Bake about an hour, until a toothpick inserted in the center comes out clean. Cool in the pan 10 minutes and turn out on a rack to cool thoroughly. Wrap well and store. It is better the second day.

KENTUCKY MILK & HONEY LOAF

- 1 cup graham flour
- 2 tsp. baking powder
- ½ tsp. salt
- 1 cup flour
- 1 cup milk
- ½ cup dark honey

Butter a 7x3 loaf pan. Preheat oven to 375°. Put the graham flour in a mixing bowl. Over it sift the regular flour, baking powder, and salt. Measure the milk in a 2-cup measure and incorporate the honey at a drizzle. Pour into the flour, beat until well combined. Turn into prepared pan and bake 40–50 minutes, until humped and well browned. Eat warm or cooled, with lots of butter; extra honey is not really needed. Keeps a day or two, well wrapped.

DARK BANANA BREAD

Banana bread has become an American staple because of its good flavor and adaptability—sandwiched with cream cheese it makes a meal, and it keeps so well it is ready for a snack or dessert whenever needed. This version includes wheat germ and whole wheat flour for extra goodness.

1 cup flour	¾ cup honey
1 cup whole wheat flour	2 eggs, beaten
¼ cup raw wheat germ	1 cup mashed bananas, *about 3, very ripe*
½ tsp. salt	2-3 Tbsp. hot water
1 tsp. baking soda	½ cup nuts, dates, or raisins, chopped
½ cup butter	

Preheat oven to 325°. Butter a 9x5 loaf pan or three small foil loaf pans. Combine the regular flour, whole wheat flour, wheat germ, salt, and soda in a medium bowl and set aside. In a large, heavy saucepan melt the butter and stir in the honey until evenly mixed and just lukewarm. Add the beaten eggs and banana, combining thoroughly. Stir in the dry ingredients in two parts, adding hot water between additions to make a light, smooth dough. Stir in nuts or fruits as desired. Push into prepared pan, level surface, and bake 70 minutes or until humped, brown, and firm to the touch. Cool in the pan on a rack. Turn out, wrap well, and store a day before slicing.

SWEET CARROT BREAD

Amazingly simple to put together, this good bread is an invitation to experiment: add different dried fruits and nuts, up to a cup more than we suggest. Try different combinations of flours and spices. The amount of honey can be reduced, and you will still have a moist, long-keeping bread. Pan sizes can be varied from large to small and baking time remains essentially the same; pay attention near the end of baking and remove bread when it is nicely rounded and springs back when gently pressed near the center. The recipe can be doubled and will make three 8x4 loaf pans.

1 cup flour	½ cup currants
1 cup whole wheat flour	½ cup pecans, chopped
2 tsp. cinnamon	2 cups carrots, grated
2 tsp. baking soda	1 cup bland oil
½ tsp. salt	1 cup honey
½ cup coconut	3 eggs
	2 tsp. vanilla

Preheat oven to 350°. Grease pans in sizes as desired. Combine the flours, soda, spices, and salt in a large mixing bowl. Add the coconut, currants, and pecans and stir together. Add grated carrots, oil, honey, eggs, and vanilla; mix thoroughly. You can bake this quantity in a 9x5 loaf; three 1-pound empty tin cans; three of the smallest available foil loaf pans. Bake about one hour, until uniformly dark and firm. Cool in pans 10 minutes; turn out to complete cooling on rack. Wrap well and age one day before eating. Keeps about two weeks refrigerated.

UPSIDE-DOWN APPLE TART

A shiny lemon glaze gives distinction to this apple tart, nice to make during the long months when other fruits are in short supply.

2 generous cups tart
  green apples, peeled
  and sliced, *about 3*
⅓ cup honey
a few gratings of nutmeg
grated rind and juice
  of one lemon
1 Tbsp. flour
2 Tbsp. butter

1 cup flour
½ cup sugar
1 tsp. baking powder
¼ tsp. salt
¼ cup milk
1 egg plus 1 egg yolk
1 Tbsp. melted butter

Preheat oven to 425°. Butter heavily a 10″ pyrex pie plate. Place the peeled, sliced apples in a large bowl. Combine the honey, nutmeg, lemon rind, lemon juice, and 1 Tbsp. flour and pour over the apples, stirring well to coat all pieces. Arrange the apple slices in neat circles on the bottom of the pie plate, pouring any honey-lemon mixture left in the bowl over them. Dot with 2 Tbsp. butter. Sift together the flour, sugar, baking powder, and salt, into a mixing bowl. In a measuring cup combine the milk, egg yolks, and melted butter. Add to the dry ingredients and stir until blended. Carefully spread the batter over the apples. Bake 25–30 minutes until the top is browned and the fruit is golden and bubbly. Cool in the pan a few minutes, then reverse onto a platter before the honey glaze hardens. Serve warm, either plain or with sweetened whipped cream.

WARM BRAN COFFEECAKE

The mud-pie mixing method used here sometimes produces a pudding plus sauce, but in this recipe it yields a tender, extra-moist cake. It is best eaten warm; half a recipe can be baked in an 8x4 pan, and this will avoid any potential leftover problem. Good for breakfast or dessert.

1 cup raw wheat bran or all-bran cereal	½ tsp. salt
1 cup milk	5 Tbsp. sugar
¼ cup butter	3 Tbsp. orange juice
2 Tbsp. honey	6 Tbsp. honey
grated rind of a small orange	1 cup water
¼ cup broken nuts	¼ cup butter
1 cup flour	
2 tsp. baking powder	

Soak the bran in the milk in a large mixing bowl for a few minutes. Add soft butter and 2 Tbsp. honey and mix well. Grate the orange rind directly into the bowl (so that all the aromatic oils spray into the batter) and add nuts. Sift together flour, baking powder, salt, and sugar, and stir in until just moistened. Push this mixture into a well-buttered 8″ square pan. Bring the orange juice, 6 Tbsp. honey, water, and butter to a boil in a small saucepan and pour over the batter. Bake at 350° 40–45 minutes (use the same timing for half a recipe) until brown. Serve warm.

HONEY NUT CRUMBCAKE

This coffeecake lends itself to two-stage preparation; the dry crumb mixture can be mixed the night before and the buttermilk, honey, and egg set out so that in the morning you are half an hour from a fresh, tasty hot bread. Portions can be reheated, wrapped in foil in a 350° oven.

¾ cup butter
1 cup light brown sugar
½ tsp. salt
½ tsp. cinnamon
½ tsp. nutmeg, freshly grated
2¼ cups flour
¾ cup walnuts, broken
1 tsp. baking soda
½ tsp. baking powder
1 egg
1 cup buttermilk
¾ cup honey

Preheat oven to 350°. Grease a 9x13 baking pan. Cream together the soft butter and brown sugar in a large mixing bowl. Add the salt, cinnamon, nutmeg, and flour, mixing with your fingertips until uniform, non-sticky crumbs are formed. Set aside ½ cup of this mixture and add the walnuts to it; this will be the topping. To the remaining dry ingredients add soda and baking powder. In a large measuring cup combine the buttermilk, honey, and egg; stir into the flour mixture until all ingredients are moist. Spread in prepared pan and sprinkle the reserved nut crumbs over the top, pressing in gently. Bake 25–30 minutes, until top springs back when gently pressed and it has begun to shrink from the sides of the pan. Serve warm, cut from the pan.

SQUASH CORNBREAD

Bright color and extra moistness result from the use of squash in this recipe. We suspect that pumpkin and sweet potato would do very nicely, too.

1 cup buttermilk	¾ cup mashed squash,
1 tsp. baking soda	at room temperature
1 cup sour cream	2 cups corn meal
2 Tbsp. honey	1½ tsp. salt
2 eggs	1½ Tbsp. butter

Preheat oven to 350°. Dissolve the soda in the buttermilk. Stir in the sour cream and incorporate the honey in a thin stream. In a medium mixing bowl beat the eggs, add the squash, corn meal, salt, and liquid mixture. In a 9″ pie plate or baking dish melt 1½ Tbsp. butter; tilt the pan to coat the dish well and pour the excess in the batter (1 Tbsp.). Stir in, pour into baking dish. Bake 30–40 minutes, until set at the center. Serve hot with lots of butter. Also excellent toasted the next day, with butter and honey.

FLAKY BISCUITS

Biscuits and honey are ubiquitous in meals of the American South. At times I have felt they must sustain life on their own, because even on the steamiest summer day biscuits companion plates of overcooked greens, slabs of potato, and meat with gravy—all unpalatable in the heat. The biscuits may or may not be technically refined, but they are hot and have the merit of impeccable freshness; skip the margarine that is usually offered, rely on honey to top them, and biscuits will do as survival fare. This recipe is not Southern but yields biscuits that are technically splendid. Follow the rule of impeccable freshness and serve hot with honey and real butter, please.

2 cups flour	2 eggs, well beaten
3 tsp. baking powder	½ cup cold milk
¾ tsp. salt	
½ cup plus 2 Tbsp. cold butter	

Preheat oven to 475°. Sift the flour, baking powder, and salt into a mixing bowl. With a pastry blender cut in the ½ cup butter until the mixture has the texture of meal. In a large measuring cup measure ½ cup milk, drop in the eggs, and beat together. Pour this into the flour and mix together with a fork, lightly; it is better to have a few loose flour particles than to overmix. On a floured board roll this dough into a rectangle half an inch thick. Over the lower two-thirds of the dough distribute the 2 Tbsp. butter cut into small pieces. Work quickly so the butter does not warm up. Fold the upper third over the middle of the dough and the lower third over that. Turn this rectangle halfway round on the board, roll again to ½" thick, and fold and roll again. Cut the ½" thick dough into squares 1½" across and place them, slightly separated, on an ungreased baking sheet. Bake about 10 minutes, until puffed and brown.

VARIATION: These are great split and served with crushed berries as shortcake; cut into desired serving shapes and bake as directed.

BANNOCK: A SCOTTISH OATCAKE

Scottish soldiers of medieval times fortified themselves on long treks by preparing simple cakes of oats and water baked on a small griddle over a wood fire. Similar cakes, called bannocks, are made throughout Scotland today enriched with butter, cream, and honey, sustenance for blustery winter mornings. Much-prized heather honey would be especially appropriate here. If oat flour is not available, grind whole oats in a coffee mill.

½ cup butter	1 Tbsp. warm water
2 cups oat flour	⅓ cup cream
3 Tbsp. honey, preferably heather	½ tsp. salt

Preheat oven to 325°. Butter a 9x9 square pan. Using a pastry blender, cut the butter into the oat flour until the mixture has a uniform mealy texture. Dilute the honey with the water and combine in a measuring cup with the cream and salt. Add to the oat mixture, stirring with a fork until thoroughly blended. Press the dough into the prepared pan. Crease the top into 12 squares. Dot each with a little extra butter. Bake for 12 minutes, until the surface looks dry and lightly browned. Remove and let cool in the pan on a rack. These are extremely fragile while hot; cool at least 20 minutes before removing from pan. Transfer carefully with a spatula to a serving plate; while oatcakes need no topping, they are best served with a cup of fresh strong tea.

CALIFORNIA MUFFINS

Nutty with wheat germ, these muffins do a great deal to make a meal festive and wholesome.

1 cup sifted flour
1 tsp. baking powder
¼ tsp. baking soda
½ tsp. salt
½ cup raw wheat germ
¼ cup butter, at room temperature

¼ cup honey, preferably orange blossom
1 egg, beaten
grated rind of one orange
½ cup orange juice

Preheat oven to 375°. Butter a muffin tin or popover pan. Sift the flour with the baking powder, soda, and salt; set aside. Cream the butter, then add the honey and beat until smooth and fluffy. Blend in the egg, orange rind, and orange juice. Add the dry ingredients to the creamed mixture, stirring with a wooden spoon just until al' the ingredients are moist. The batter will look lumpy. Fill greased tins ⅔ full and bake for 20 minutes, until rounded and brown. Turn out immediately, bundle in a cloth-lined basket, and bring to the table. Offer butter and honey to top them.

HONEY BRAN MUFFINS

The best bran muffins ever.

1 cup flour
3 cups whole bran
1 tsp. baking powder
½ tsp. baking soda
1 tsp. salt
⅓ cup butter, at
room temperature

¼ cup brown sugar,
packed
¼ cup honey
1 egg
⅞ cup buttermilk
(1 cup minus 2 Tbsp.)

Preheat oven to 400°. Grease a muffin tin or popover pan. Blend the flour, bran, baking powder, soda, and salt and set aside. This may be done the night before to minimize preparation time in the morning, if they are to be breakfast muffins. Cream the butter, sugar, honey, and egg. Stir in the dry ingredients alternately with the buttermilk, just until all ingredients are moistened; avoid beating. Fill prepared pans ⅔ full; drizzle about a teaspoon honey over the top of each muffin. Bake 20–25 minutes. Turn out of pans immediately and serve hot with butter. Makes 12 muffins.

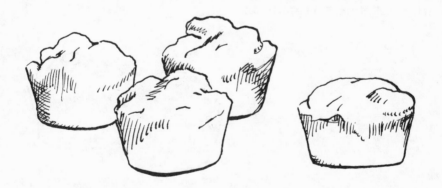

WHOLE WHEAT BERRY MUFFINS

A basic muffin to be varied according to the fruit of the season. Wheat germ is a nice addition; substitute for an equal amount of flour. Serve muffins fresh from the oven; these lend themselves to a topping of honey as well as butter. Additional honey can be added to the batter if a sweeter bread is preferred.

1 cup whole wheat flour	1 Tbsp. honey
1½ tsp. baking powder	1 egg
½ tsp. salt	½ cup sour cream
½ cup blueberries	2-4 Tbsp. buttermilk

Preheat oven to 375°. Butter a muffin tin or popover pan. Sift together into a medium mixing bowl the flour, baking powder, and salt. Toss the berries lightly through this mixture; this will keep them from sinking to the bottom. In a large measuring cup, measure the sour cream and add the egg and honey, mixing all together. Add to the dry ingredients, combining lightly. Add buttermilk, 2–4 Tbsp. as needed to make a soft dough. Spoon into the prepared tin and bake 20–25 minutes, until golden and firm to a gentle touch. Serve hot with butter and honey. ❧ ❧ For extra lightness, separate the egg and add the yolk with the cream as directed; beat the egg white until stiff and fold in as the last step.

VARIATION: Substitute drained canned cherries, raspberries, or chopped sweetened cranberries instead of blueberries.

TUNISIAN ORANGE DOUGHNUTS
with honey syrup

An unusual breakfast treat, easy to prepare if one has an extra half hour one morning and a jar of basic honey syrup on hand. The doughnuts are best eaten at once. Provide plenty of napkins for your guests, since they are sticky.

2 eggs	2 cups flour
¼ cup bland oil	1 Tbsp. baking soda
¼ cup sugar	oil for deep frying
¼ cup orange juice	1 cup Basic Honey
grated rind of one	Syrup, *see recipe*
orange	

Combine the eggs, oil, sugar, orange juice, and orange rind in a medium bowl, stirring until smooth. Sift the flour with the baking soda and add to the first mixture, beating constantly. Continue beating until the mixture is thick and falls from the spoon in a ribbon. Cover and set aside for about 30 minutes. Heat the oil in a deep saucepan to 350°. The oil should be deep but should not fill the pan, lest it bubble over the sides when the doughnuts are added. While oil is heating, warm the cup of Basic Honey Syrup. To shape the doughnuts, flour your hands heavily and gather the dough into a ball. Divide into 12 equal parts. In your hands roll each part into a ball, flatten it in your palm, and poke a hole through the middle with a finger. Keep hands well floured to prevent sticking. Fry the doughnuts without crowding for 3 to 5 minutes, turning once, until golden brown. Drain on paper towels. When all doughnuts are cooked and drained, prick them in two or three places with a fork, pick them up with tongs and dip them into the warmed honey syrup. Eat at once. Makes 12 small doughnuts.

Sopaipillas

A Mexican specialty, sopaipillas are fried bread in a puffed lozenge shape especially well suited to filling with butter and honey. In the Southwest United States they might appear on the table with dinner, but they are also perfect for brunch or after a bowl of soup, when you can give your undivided attention to tearing off a corner, dousing with honey, and eating the sopaipillas hot from the pan.

2 cups flour
½ tsp. baking powder
½ tsp. salt
½ cup milk
1 egg
oil for frying

Sift the flour, baking powder, and salt into a medium bowl. Measure the ½ cup milk, drop an egg into the cup, and beat together. Add to flour, making a smooth, firm dough. If necessary for smoothness, turn out on a lightly floured board and knead a few times. Then roll out as thin as possible and cut into 2″ squares; it is easier to do about a third of the dough at a time. Meanwhile preheat a pan of bland oil or vegetable shortening at least 3″ deep to 375°. Place a few squares at a time in the hot fat so they are not crowded. The dough should sink to the bottom, inflate along its entire surface in a single blister, then rise and brown. Turn and brown the second side; this takes less time. The entire process takes only minutes. Drain as they are finished on absorbent paper and serve at once, dusted with powdered sugar. Fill with honey and eat hot.

POPPYSEED HONEY TOAST

This extremely simple formula is too good to leave out. Do not delay in serving it—these toasts are delicious only when piping hot.

    half a stick butter
    2 Tbsp. honey
    2 tsp. poppyseeds

Cream the butter with honey and poppyseeds until smooth. Toast both sides of fresh bread slices, then spread one side with the honey-butter mixture. Grill under a preheated broiler for a few minutes, until the edges start to bubble and brown. Serve at once.

RICOTTA PANCAKES

Ricotta cheese deserves to be more widely known; it is fresh and simple in taste like cottage cheese. In these pancakes it makes a tasty cheese entree.

1 cup ricotta cheese	2 tsp. honey
3 eggs	¼ tsp. salt
2 Tbsp. bland oil	butter for frying
⅓ cup flour	

Combine all ingredients in a blender jar and blend until smooth, about five minutes, scraping the sides of the jar as needed. Or sieve the cheese into a bowl and beat in the remaining ingredients until smooth. Fry in 3″ cakes on a well-buttered surface over medium heat, turning when bubbles appear. Serve at once, with honey or jam.

BREAD-CRUMB PANCAKES

While this recipe might appear the last resource of a frugal housewife, the pancakes actually make the most of any good, if stale, bread you might have on hand. With jam and sour cream they make a nice brunch or supper. The recipe yields 24 small, delicate pancakes with a little crisp border.

1½ cups fine bread crumbs	½ tsp. salt
1½ cups milk	1 Tbsp. honey
½ cup flour	1 Tbsp. melted butter
2 tsp. baking powder	1 egg

In a medium mixing bowl cover the crumbs with milk and let soak 15 minutes. Sift the dry ingredients (flour, baking powder, salt) together, and mix the egg and liquids (honey, butter) with a fork. Combine all ingredients. Fry by the tablespoonful on a hot griddle, turning when the edge is nicely browned; only a few bubbles will appear on the surface when ready. The second side browns quickly. Serve at once, with melted butter.

NOTE: The easiest way to make breadcrumbs is in a blender, trimming off crusts and putting in 1″ cubes a third of a jar at a time. A few seconds of operation will produce uniform, fine crumbs. Some variation in crumb size is all right here, so a hand method also does well. Crumb the bread with a sharp knife, as in mincing (firm bread crumbs a little as you work). Spread the crumbs in a shallow layer in a baking pan and set in a recently turned off oven to dry out further, if needed.

HONEY ORANGE NUT WAFFLES

2 cups sifted cake flour
1 Tbsp. baking powder
1 tsp. salt
3 eggs, separated
2 Tbsp. honey
1 cup milk

¼ cup orange juice
½ cup bland oil
grated rind of one
large orange
pecans, almonds, or
walnuts, chopped

Preheat a waffle iron. Sift together the flour, baking powder, and salt and set aside. Beat the egg yolks with a wire whip, then add the honey, milk, oil, orange juice, and orange rind. Blend well. Stir in the dry ingredients, mixing until smooth. Beat the reserved egg whites until stiff but not dry. Stir one fourth of the whites into the batter to lighten it. Gently but thoroughly fold in the rest, using a rubber spatula. Ladle out onto hot waffle iron, sprinkle with nuts, and bake. Waffles are done when the steam stops appearing at the sides; they should be golden and crisp. Serve with Honey Butter (see recipe) or other toppings as desired.

Buttermilk WHOLE WHEAT PANCAKES

Thanks to the whole wheat flour, these pancakes are very satisfying and make a nutritious quick meal. Fruits of the season can be used to vary them. Half a recipe will make a hearty meal for one.

1 scant cup whole
wheat flour
1 ½ tsp. baking powder
½ tsp. salt
2 egg yolks

1 Tbsp. honey
2 Tbsp. melted butter
1 cup buttermilk, *or more*
2 egg whites

Mix the dry ingredients in a medium bowl. Beat the egg yolks, add the honey, butter, and buttermilk. Add the liquid to the dry ingredients. Gently fold in the egg whites, beaten until stiff but not dry. These proportions yield thick, tender pancakes (about 8). Add more buttermilk if thinner pancakes are preferred. Bake on a medium-hot griddle, well buttered, turning when bubbles appear on the batter surface. Serve with honey.

VARIATION: Blueberry pancakes. Follow the recipe, stirring one cup dry blueberries into the dry ingredients after they are combined. The pancakes should be fried a little slower than plain ones. They are especially good served with sour cream sweetened with just a little honey.

GRANOLA

One of the food hits of the decade, granola is a mixture of whole grains and natural sweets that appealed instantly to people looking for healthful, nourishing snack food. Making your own granola encourages you to adapt the basic formula to suit your taste preference—in addition to the fundamental rolled oats, you can add other grains, nuts, seeds, and fruits. The gentle oven roasting seems to bring each element to peak flavor, at the same time blending the parts into an interesting whole.

2 cups rolled oats	¼ cup whole bran
½ cup raw wheat germ	¼ cup soy oil
½ cup chopped cashews	¼ cup honey
½ cup hulled sunflower seeds	¼ tsp. vanilla
	½ cup raisins
¼ cup sesame seeds	

Preheat oven to 325°. Combine the grains and nuts in a large mixing bowl. In a small saucepan heat the oil, honey, and vanilla, stirring to blend well. Pour over the dry ingredients and mix thoroughly. Spread in an even layer in a jelly roll pan and toast about 20 minutes, turning the mixture with a spatula every five minutes to prevent sticking and encourage even browning. Remove from oven when nicely browned and stir in the raisins. Stir once or twice while cooling. Store in a 5-pound honey tin or other suitable container. Eat with milk as a cereal, or use as an out-of-hand snack.

SWISS BREAKFAST *muesli*

This mixture of grains, fruits, and nuts was originally a health diet dish created by Dr. Bircher-Benner for patients in his Zurich clinic at the turn of the century. Now enjoyed throughout the world, Muesli was preferred by nutrition-conscious people over other cereals long before granola was invented. But most people know the packaged version only, which necessarily lacks the fresh flavor of homemade. As with granola, ingredients can be varied to suit taste preferences and to use the fruits of the season. For each serving:

  1 Tbsp. oatmeal, soaked overnight in 3 Tbsp. water
  1 Tbsp. raw wheat germ or whole bran
  ½ Tbsp. lemon juice
  1 Tbsp. milk or yogurt sweetened with 1 Tbsp. honey
  1 large unpeeled apple
  1 Tbsp. chopped almonds or hazelnuts

To serve, stir the wheat germ, lemon juice, and sweetened milk into the soaked oatmeal. Grate the apple directly into the mixture, stir, and sprinkle with chopped nuts.

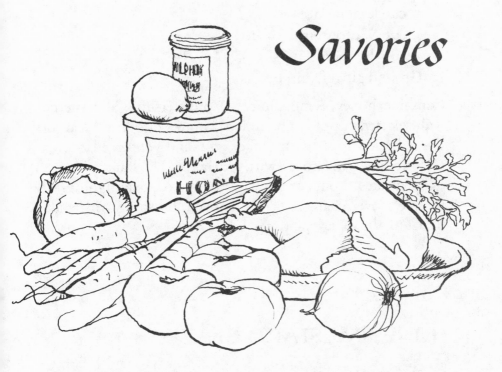

Savories

A modest selection is given here of recipes for main dishes and vegetables complemented by the use of honey. Too many formulas are in currency for heavy sweet glazes and sauces that overwhelm the natural flavor of vegetables and meats they are served with. Balance and restraint are essential in these savory combinations.

Honey has a place in cooking with vegetables, where by adding just a few drops the faded flavor of store-bought carrots or beets can be improved. Root vegetables of all kinds, rutabagas, parsnips, sweet potatoes, many squashes and pumpkin, corn, and beans of all kinds have a special affinity for honey.

LAMB MARINADE

½ cup honey
¼ cup lemon juice
¼ cup Worcestershire sauce
¼ cup dry sherry
   Ground ginger, salt, pepper

Combine honey, lemon juice, Worcestershire, and sherry. Rub selected cut of lamb (riblets, chunks of boned meat, or round-bone chops) with ginger, salt, and pepper. Place in a ceramic bowl and cover with marinade. Let stand at room temperature 4 hours or refrigerate, covered, overnight. Grill the meat over charcoal or in the oven, brushing with additional marinade several times.

HONEY-MUSTARD GLAZE

2 Tbsp. Dijon-type mustard
¼ cup honey
2 Tbsp. brown sugar

Combine ingredients in a small saucepan and bring to a boil. Simmer about five minutes, stirring frequently. Preheat broiler. Place a cooked corned beef brisket or a fat slice of ham on a broiler rack; brush with the glaze. Broil six inches from heat for 10 minutes, brushing twice with additional glaze. Serve at once.

FRESH HERB SALAD DRESSING

This dressing may be used on mixed green salads or may be passed in a side dish to spoon over fresh cucumber and tomato.

½ cup yogurt
1 Tbsp. honey
½ Tbsp. lemon juice
1 Tbsp. green onion, finely chopped
½ Tbsp. parsley, finely chopped

½ tsp. salt
¼ tsp. fresh oregano, marjoram, tarragon, or basil, finely chopped

Combine all ingredients and blend thoroughly. Chill before serving; use within a day or two. Use any fresh herbs you have growing—do not substitute dried herbs.

CURRY SALAD DRESSING

Made without oil, this is a refreshing dressing for those who watch calories or cholesterol.

½ cup orange juice
2 Tbsp. honey
2 Tbsp. cider vinegar
2 Tbsp. sweet pickle juice
1 tsp. curry powder

Shake all ingredients together in a covered jar; serve on fruit salad. Best when freshly made.

LAMB BRAISED WITH FRUIT & HONEY
Tajine, fez style

Some of the outstanding dishes of Middle Eastern cooking are meats and fruits simmered until a rich sauce is formed, served with rice or couscous. This tajine, a specialty of Fez, further heightens flavor by adding honey in the last minutes of cooking, but the sweetness is balanced by spices and pungent black pepper. Many variations on the dish are possible, and since it is easily prepared and succulent it makes a worthy experiment. This dish is best presented in the Eastern fashion, as one of several entrees in a meal of many courses.

3 pounds leg of lamb, in 1″ cubes	1 onion, finely chopped
2 Tbsp. oil	water
¼ tsp. ginger	3 green apples, peeled and cored, in chunks
½ tsp. ground coriander	2 Tbsp. honey
1 tsp. cinnamon	toasted sesame seeds, for garnish
salt	
freshly ground pepper	

Place the lamb, oil, spices, and onion in a heavy stove-to-oven casserole. Add water almost to the level of the meat. Bring to a boil, cover, and simmer very gently for two hours. If the sauce is thin, drain it from the pot and place in a large pan, so that there is maximum surface; boil rapidly to reduce to about 2 cups. Return to the meat, add chunks of apple, and simmer 20 minutes; they will cook in the steam. Watch carefully so they do not get mushy, and a few minutes before they are done, add the honey. Taste sauce and re-season, adding more pepper or salt as required. Season highly, because the sauce will not taste as strong when eaten with the meat and rice. Serve at once, sprinkled with toasted sesame seeds and accompanied by Persian rice or steamed couscous.

VARIATION: Instead of the apples, add ½ pound prunes and finish as directed. This should cook down to a thick, rich sauce. OR add saffron, about ¼ tsp., instead of coriander. OR instead of the apples, use well-drained sour red cherries. When they are tender, mash the cherries with the back of a spoon so they further combine into the sauce.

FAR EASTERN CHICKEN

6 whole chicken breasts, skins removed
1 Tbsp. cinnamon
½ Tbsp. curry powder
1 tsp. salt
1 clove garlic, minced
½ cup honey
¾ cup unsweetened grapefruit juice
1 cup crushed pineapple

Place chicken breasts in a single layer in a large frying pan. Combine the honey, cinnamon, curry powder, salt, and garlic in a large measuring cup. Stir in the grapefruit juice, blending well. Pour over the chicken. Cover the pan and simmer over medium heat for 20 minutes, stirring to prevent sticking and turning the chicken once. Preheat broiler. When the chicken is tender, transfer to a broiler-proof serving dish. Combine the pan juices with pineapple and spread this mixture evenly over the chicken pieces. Broil six inches from the heat for 5 minutes, or until lightly glazed and bubbling. Serve with steamed rice.

GLAZED PORK LOIN ROAST

4-5 pound loin of pork,
    about 10 chops
2 tsp. salt
   freshly ground pepper

1 cup orange juice
⅓ cup honey
1 Tbsp. ginger
¼ tsp. ground cloves

Preheat oven to 325°. Rub the pork roast with salt and pepper and place fat side up in a roasting pan. Cook 2½ to 3 hours, or until 180° on a meat thermometer placed in the flesh of the roast. Meanwhile combine the orange juice, honey, ginger, and cloves in a small saucepan and simmer 30 minutes. During the last hour of cooking, brush the roast several times with this mixture to produce a shiny glaze. Serve with rice pilaff or black beans.

SAVORY SOYBEANS

Protein-rich baked soybeans are an excellent, inexpensive main dish.

1½ cups dry soybeans
2 small tomatoes,
   chopped
½ cup tomato sauce
1 small green pepper,
   seeded and chopped
3 green onions, chopped,
   including the tops
3 slices bacon, diced

3 Tbsp. honey
1 Tbsp. dry mustard
1 tsp. salt,
   more if needed
   freshly ground pepper

The night before, place the soybeans in a 3-quart kettle. Add water to one inch above the beans. Cover and soak overnight.

The next day, drain beans, discarding any loose husks, and return to kettle. Preheat oven to 325°. Combine the beans with all the remaining ingredients, adding water to barely cover. Bring to a boil on top of the stove, cover, then place the pan in the oven and bake for 4 hours, until tender. The beans should be a tawny color, the liquid reduced by one half. If you prefer dryer beans, bake another hour. Nice to serve with Squash Corn Bread (see recipe) and a fresh cucumber-yogurt salad. The beans improve in flavor if made in advance and reheated.

DRIED LIMA BEAN CASSEROLE

1 pound dried lima beans
1 onion, diced
1 green pepper, diced
1 clove garlic, crushed
1 tomato, diced

3 Tbsp. honey
salt
freshly ground pepper
3 strips bacon

Soak the lima beans overnight in a large cooking pot in water to cover by two inches. Next day, simmer them in the water for 30 minutes. Preheat oven to 350°. Fry the bacon, cut into small pieces, and remove from the pan, leaving the fat. Saute the vegetables gently in the bacon fat until soft; off the heat, stir in the honey, salt, and pepper. Lift the lima beans from the cooking liquor and add to the skillet, mixing all together; pour into 1½ quart baking dish, adding liquid to come almost to the top of the beans. Taste for seasoning; use enough pepper so that the dish is spicy. Bake about 40 minutes, adding liquid if needed; in the final 5 minutes, top with the reserved bacon bits. Serve at once.

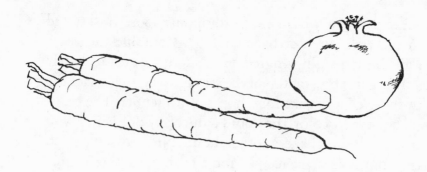

CARROTS IN POMEGRANATE SAUCE

From early times people of the arid Middle East have esteemed the pomegranate for its refreshing juice. King Solomon had an orchard of pomegranates; Mohammed himself recommended eating a pomegranate in order to purge oneself of envy and hatred. Chicken braised with pomegranate juice and walnuts is a great Iranian specialty. With vegetables, the juice provides the essential tang that balances a sweet glaze.

1 bunch fresh carrots (5–6 medium)	1½ tsp. potato starch flour
3 Tbsp. butter, or more	honey to taste
½ cup bottled pomegranate juice	

Peel the carrots and cut into sticks; cook with butter in a tightly covered skillet until tender, as much as 45 minutes. Add more butter if desired. Stir the potato starch flour into the juice until smooth and sweeten to taste with honey. Combine the sauce with the butter-cooked carrots and heat, stirring, until the sauce thickens and carrots are well coated.

VARIATION: Use the same sauce on small whole beets or sliced beets.

CHILLED CHERRY & BEET SOUP

Cold soups are commonplace in European menus, and they deserve attention from anyone who would like more choices for beginning a meal. This version has something special added: sour cherries, dyed purple by the beet juice.

5 or 6 small fresh beets
1 onion
1 cup sour red cherries, canned
3 whole cloves

2 Tbsp. honey
2 Tbsp. lemon juice
salt

Grate the beets or slice thinly; slice the onion thin. Cook the vegetables in 5 cups water about 30 minutes. Meanwhile simmer the cherries with cloves in one cup water for 5 minutes. Drain the beets, discarding the vegetable pulp, and combine the strained liquid with the cherries and their liquid. Season with honey, lemon juice, and salt. The sweet-sour balance should not be tasted distinctly, but serves to enhance the other flavors. Serve with sour cream as a first course. Serves 6.

PICKLED BEETS

8 small beets, boiled and peeled
⅓ cup red wine
¼ cup tarragon wine vinegar

2 Tbsp. honey
1 tsp. ground cloves
1 tsp. cinnamon
salt and pepper

Slice the cooked, peeled beets and place in a glass serving dish. In a small saucepan bring the remaining ingredients to a boil; cook one minute. Pour this marinade over the beets and stir to distribute evenly. Cool and chill in the refrigerator for several hours. Serve the beets as they are or arrange them in rows on a salad platter with slices of fresh garden cucumbers. Pass a separate bowl of yogurt or Fresh Herb Dressing.

HONEY-CIDER SLAW

In New Hampshire vinegar means only one thing: apple cider vinegar, used liberally on cooked parsnips and sliced cucumbers. In this slaw it makes a particularly pleasing sweet-sour combination with honey. The slaw would often be served in side dishes with hot dogs, baked beans, and cornbread.

1 large head cabbage, *2 pounds*	1 Tbsp. salt
	1 tsp. dry mustard
2 medium yellow onions	⅔ cup bland oil
¼ cup sugar	1 cup apple cider
¼ cup honey	vinegar
2 tsp. brown sugar	1 tsp. celery seed

Quarter, core, and shred the cabbage. Place in a very large bowl. Peel the onions and slice them paper thin. Arrange in a layer on top of the cabbage. Sprinkle with sugar and drizzle with honey, without stirring. Combine the remaining ingredients in a small saucepan and bring to a boil. Pour over the cabbage and onions. Stir everything together and let stand at least four hours. As the slaw marinates its apparent volume will shrink by at least a half. Transfer to a glass serving dish and store, covered, in the refrigerator. Use as needed; it will keep two weeks.

TOMATO SHERBET

Honey enhances the fresh tomato flavor without making it unnaturally sweet, creating a sherbet that is extraordinarily tasty and beautiful.

3 cups tomato puree (about 8 large ripe tomatoes)

3 Tbsp. lemon juice

1 Tbsp. onion juice (squeeze in a garlic press)

2 Tbsp. honey

½ tsp. ground fennel seed

½ tsp. salt

¼ tsp. pepper

Peel, seed, and puree the tomatoes through the finest grate of a food mill. If you cannot find ripe tomatoes, substitute top-quality canned tomato juice, reducing it by boiling until slightly thickened. Add the remaining ingredients to the puree, adjust seasoning, pour into a freezer tray, cover with plastic wrap, and freeze until quite firm. If it is frozen solid, allow the sherbet to soften at room temperature for half an hour before serving. Scoop into avocado halves and garnish with fresh green herbs.

DEVILED CARROTS

one bunch carrots, about six

¼ cup butter

2 tsp. honey

¼ tsp. salt

½ tsp. dry mustard

freshly ground pepper

In a large frying pan with a cover melt the butter. Add carrots, which have been peeled and cut into even julienne strips; sprinkle with salt, cover tightly, and steam in the butter until tender, 15–30 minutes. Combine the honey, mustard, and salt and add to the pan, stirring with frequent turning to coat evenly. Simmer a few minutes and serve at once.

CORN FRITTERS

10 oz. package frozen corn	½ tsp. salt
1 Tbsp. water	freshly ground pepper
1 Tbsp. butter	1 tsp. honey
¼ cup milk	1-2 tsp. chopped fresh
1 egg	chives
½ cup flour	shortening for frying
½ tsp. baking powder	

Place the frozen corn, water, and butter in a saucepan that can be tightly covered; over high heat bring to a boil; reduce heat, add milk, cover and simmer until tender, about 5 minutes. Drain and cool, reserving liquid. Beat the egg in a small bowl and add flour, baking powder, salt, pepper, honey, and the reserved corn milk. Stir in 1½ cups corn and the snipped chives. Heat the shortening for frying in a large fry pan, allowing one inch depth; the fritters should brown in about three minutes per side, about 400°. Fry the batter by the tablespoonful, allowing ample space so that crowding does not prevent even cooking. Add liquid or flour as needed to make lacy cakes. Fry until brown, turn, and remove to paper towels to drain when brown and crisp. Serve hot with additional honey. A pleasant accompaniment to pork sausages or Canadian bacon, for brunch or supper. Makes 16–20 fritters.

ENGLISH PARSNIP PIE

In New England parsnips are allowed to remain in the ground all winter, to be dug in the spring when the first thaws permit, their flavor enhanced by the long freezing. For those who think that parsnips need more than freezing to make them palatable, this traditional English savory may be the answer.

Pastry for an 8 inch
  two-crust pie
1 pound parsnips
1 tsp. salt
3 Tbsp. honey
⅛ tsp. ginger
¼ tsp. cinnamon

¼ tsp. freshly-grated
  orange rind
dash of mace
1½ tsp. lemon juice
2 egg yolks, lightly
  beaten

Preheat oven to 450°. Peel the parsnips and boil in lightly salted water until tender enough to pierce easily with a fork. Meanwhile line an 8 inch removable-bottom tart pan with pastry, trimming the top edges by running a rolling pin over the pan. Roll out the remaining pastry and cut into 8 strips ½" wide to use for a lattice top. Bake the shell for 5 minutes, remove from oven, and set aside on a rack. When the parsnips are done, drain and run through the finest grate of a food mill. Add the seasonings, lemon juice, and egg yolks and blend thoroughly. Pour into the partly baked pastry shell. Weave a lattice top, pressing the ends of the strips over the edge of the pan to trim and seal. Bake for 20 minutes or until the pastry is lightly browned. Let cool for 10 minutes before removing the outer edge of the pan. Serve warm. Parsnip pie should seem no more unlikely than sweet potato pie. In fact it does nicely as an accompaniment to roast pork, ham, or game. In Colonial America it might have appeared with a brace of ducklings, clotted cream and honey following as dessert.

Sweets

Holidays in the western world are associated with a wonderful fragrance composed of spices, fruit peels, butter and eggs,
nuts, raisins and currants, honey and molasses—it is the stuff
that gingerbread is made from, and for centuries such honey
cakes have signalled Christmas, as well as other seasonal
festival days. In the Middle Ages spices travelled to commercial centers in Germany, Poland, the Balkans, the Ukraine,
and they were baked with local honey and treasured citrus
fruits into soft loaves and firm cakes in formulas and shapes
that became traditional for each region. Because honey and

spices both added a preservative quality to the baked goods, they could be made months ahead and stored for special occasions. The ritual involved in preparing traditional foods, decorating and storing them, and sharing with friends on festival days is, fortunately, still enjoyed. A sample is offered here for cakes and cookies from many cultures: German/Swiss *lebkuchen* and *leckerli*, Lithuanian *grybai*, Bulgarian *medeni kurabi*, Italian *pignoli*, Greek *finikia*, Polish *ciastka miodow*, Canadian nut wafers, Ukrainian *medivnyk*, Estonian *mee kook*, and others.

Honey was very likely the original sweet—to judge from the enthusiasm of bears for a succulent comb, enjoyment of honey may antedate man. Since the earliest sweetened porridges and primitive sweetened breads, all manner of honeyed desserts have evolved. The best of these sweets, we believe, use honey to complement other flavors. It is especially compatible in richly spiced cookies and cakes in the European tradition, but honey also finds a place in many conventional American dishes—it is an excellent foil for tart berries in puddings and pies, it makes cookies that keep well, and it is stunning in ice cream. Cranberry or blueberry steamed puddings are sweetened with honey and delicious topped with a honey hard sauce or hot lemon sauce. Pumpkin pies, raisin pies, lemon-filled gingerbread, cardamon-apple tart are a few of the rewards of the autumn harvest. Everyday honey cookies can be soft or crisp—nutmeg coconut squares, bran or peanut-butter cookies; in any case they are well suited to store, since they keep and mellow for days or a week. Honey gives the final touch to an unusual pumpkin custard, its subtlety best appreciated at room temperature. Cardamon cake and honey ice cream offer a very special taste experience, simple but not commonplace.

Confections in the Middle East are often dipped or soaked in a honey syrup, making rich pastries that are best served in the Eastern fashion, as a special treat with a cup of hot tea; they may be overwhelming at the conclusion of a meal. In *baklava* and *kadaife,* the syrup permeates crisp nut-filled pastries; *karidopeta,* a portable loaf, is a soaked ground-nut cake to be considered for picnics. Honey complements delicate cheeses in Italian ricotta tart; *tyropeta,* a molded cheese to serve with fruit; and Greek honey pie. *Ekmek kadaif,* simply bread and syrup, is most unctuous of all.

Fresh fruits in simple combinations with honey become special desserts—we have suggested just a few of the infinite variety of possibilities. Wine, lemon juice, liqueurs, and spices give mixtures an extra lift. Honey and yogurt enjoy a special affinity for each other, creating a complete and satisfying meal with the addition of fruit or nuts.

Finally, honey combines with butter or whipped cream in various toppings—just a dollop transforms a plain pancake or a piece of toast.

Honey sweets have delighted people around the world for centuries; they are part of the cultural heritage of everyone who enjoys good tastes. For those who would become honey-eaters, this collection of recipes should stimulate cooking and baking, sampling and tasting that leads to further enjoyment of the legendary taste of honey.

FAT HONEY COOKIES

It is always nice to have on hand a simple, delicious cookie that will please a child or make a filling snack. These spice cookies are good candidates for the perpetual jar: they contain little sugar, keep remarkably because of the honey, and they are easily mixed and shaped.

4	cups flour	½	tsp. ground cloves
1½	tsp. salt	1	cup butter
1	tsp. baking soda	1¼	cups honey
1	tsp. baking powder	¼	cup sugar
2	tsp. cinnamon	1	egg
2	tsp. ginger		

Sift the flour with the salt, soda, baking powder, and spices; set aside. Melt the butter in a large, heavy saucepan with the honey and sugar. Cool to lukewarm. Beat in the egg. Add the flour mixture in several additions, beating briefly. If the dough is not easy to handle, chill it. Preheat the oven to 350°; lightly grease baking sheets. Shape the cookies by rolling in your palms to 1½" balls. Place on baking sheets about 2" apart to allow for spreading; one dozen fits well on a large baking sheet. Bake 15 minutes, until lightly browned. Remove from pans at once and cool on racks. Store in airtight tins. Makes 4 dozen.

WHOLE WHEAT NUT COOKIES

Here is a basic formula for crisp cookies, not very sweet and easily made. Combinations of many chopped dried fruits and nuts can replace the cup of walnuts.

1 cup whole wheat flour	⅜ cup honey
½ tsp. baking soda	½ tsp. vanilla
½ tsp. salt	1 egg
⅓ cup melted butter	1 cup walnuts, chopped

Preheat oven to 375°. Sift flour, soda, and salt together into a small mixing bowl. Combine the butter, honey, and vanilla and stir in. Beat the egg; mix into batter and stir in walnuts. Drop by the teaspoonful on ungreased baking sheets. Bake about 10 minutes, until lightly browned. Cool on racks. About 3 dozen.

CRISP HONEY BRAN COOKIES

All those soft brown honey cookies you have tasted to the contrary, these all-honey cookies stay crisp a long time.

2 cups flour	¼ tsp. allspice
1 tsp. baking soda	¼ cup bran flakes
½ tsp. cinnamon	½ cup butter
¼ tsp. ground cloves	½ cup honey

Sift together the flour, soda, and spices. Crush the bran flakes by rolling between two layers of waxed paper; measure and add to the flour mixture. Set aside. Cream the butter; add the honey and beat until the mixture is smooth and fluffy. Stir in the dry ingredients and blend thoroughly. Cover and chill the dough an hour, or until firm enough to roll. Preheat oven to 350°. Grease baking sheets lightly. Divide the dough in half, leaving one part in the refrigerator. Roll out ⅛" thick on a floured board and cut into 2" rounds or simple shapes. Place an inch apart on baking sheets and bake 8–10 minutes, until browned around the edges. Cool on racks. If you wish, sandwich the cookies while still warm with apricot jam. Makes 3 dozen.

CITRUS HONEY TEACAKES

½ cup butter
¼ cup honey
1 egg yolk
1 tsp. vanilla
grated rind of
    one orange

grated rind of
    one lemon
1 cup flour
½ cup pecans, finely
    chopped

Cream the butter and add the honey, egg yolk, and vanilla, mixing until light. Grate the fruit rinds directly into the bowl so no aromatic oils are lost. Work in the flour and chopped pecans. Wrap and chill for an hour, until easy to shape. Preheat oven to 325°. Form into small balls and place an inch apart on an ungreased baking sheet. Bake 15–20 minutes, until just golden brown. Cool on racks.

HONEY PEANUT-BUTTER COOKIES

1¼ cups flour
½ tsp. baking powder
¾ tsp. baking soda
¼ tsp. salt
¼ cup butter

½ cup old-fashioned
    unhomogenized crunchy
    peanut butter
½ cup sugar
½ cup honey

Sift the flour, baking powder, soda, and salt into a small bowl and set aside. In a large bowl beat the butter, peanut butter, sugar, honey, and egg until well blended. Add the dry ingredients and mix thoroughly. Cover and chill two hours. Preheat oven to 375°. Grease baking sheets lightly. Roll bits of dough into walnut-sized balls and place 2″ apart on baking sheets. Flatten with a fork dipped in flour, making a criss-cross pattern. Bake 10–12 minutes. Allow the cookies to rest on the pan a minute before transferring to a cooling rack. Makes 3 dozen.

MRS. G'S HONEY BROWNIES

A recipe from a dear New Hampshire lady who always treats visitors to an astounding array of homemade goodies.

½ cup flour	2 eggs, beaten
½ tsp. baking powder	6 Tbsp. honey
¼ tsp. salt	1 tsp. vanilla
6 ounces semi-sweet chocolate bits	1 cup chopped nuts
⅓ cup shortening	

Preheat oven to 350°. Butter an 8″ square pan. Sift the flour, baking powder, and salt into a small bowl; set aside. Melt the chocolate and shortening in a double boiler over warm, not boiling, water. Remove from heat and beat in the eggs, honey, and vanilla. Stir in the dry ingredients and nuts and beat until well blended. Spread in the prepared pan and bake 25–30 minutes. Cool in the pan and cut into squares. These are cake-like in texture, but Mrs. G. says, *If chewy kind is preferred, take out before really done.*

NUTMEG COCONUT SQUARES

1 cup cake flour
pinch salt
⅛ tsp. baking soda
½ cup sugar
¼ cup melted butter
½ tsp. nutmeg,
   freshly grated

¼ cup honey
2 egg whites
1 Tbsp. milk
¾ cup moist shredded
   coconut

Preheat oven to 350°. Butter heavily an 8″ square pan and line with waxed paper cut to fit the bottom of the pan. Sift the cake flour, salt, soda, and sugar into a mixing bowl. Stir in the remaining ingredients until thoroughly mixed, without overbeating. Pour into pan and bake 35 minutes, until top is firm to a gentle touch. Turn out onto cooling rack and remove the waxed paper; cool. Cut in squares. Store in airtight tins. Age 24 hours before serving; flavor improves with longer storage.

ENERGY BARS

Candy-like, these make an excellent addition to a child's lunch pail or in a backpack as a trail snack.

½ cup old-fashioned
   unhomogenized crunchy
   peanut butter
¼ cup honey
¼ cup water
½ cup powdered milk
½ cup raw wheat germ

½ cup shredded un-
   sweetened coconut
½ cup hulled sunflower
   seeds
½ cup chopped cashew
   nuts
½ cup sesame seeds

In a large bowl combine all ingredients, stirring to create a thick, homogeneous mass. Press into a small buttered pan or roll into a log. Wrap and chill, then slice into rounds or cut into squares. Store in airtight containers.

Nurembergers

Nurembergers carry the name of the city that acted as the center of the European spice trade during the Middle Ages. As it was also near many richly productive beekeeping districts, Nürnberg easily became a leading center of fine baking, developing the most famous honey cakes and cookies in all of Germany. These cookies are decorated with almond pieces in flower designs, and the spice bouquet is particularly zesty and delicious.

2½ cups flour	grated rind of one lemon
½ tsp. baking soda	½ cup chopped nuts
½ tsp. ground cloves	½ cup chopped candied
¾ tsp. cinnamon	orange peel, homemade
1 tsp. allspice	preferred
1 cup honey	blanched almond slices,
¾ cup light brown sugar	for decoration
1 egg	candied lemon peel,
1 Tbsp. lemon juice	for decoration

Sift together the flour, soda, and spices and set aside. In a large, heavy saucepan heat the honey and brown sugar to a boil. Cool to lukewarm. Stir in egg, lemon juice, and grate the lemon rind directly into the pan so no aromatic oils are lost. Blend in nuts and peel. Cover and chill overnight. Preheat oven to 350° and lightly grease baking sheets. Roll the dough out ¼" thick on a lightly floured board; it will be sticky. Cut into 2" circles and place one inch apart on the baking sheets. Decorate the tops with flowers of sliced nuts radiating around a bit of lemon peel. Bake 10 minutes, until edges are brown and cookies are set. Remove from pan and cool on racks. Store in airtight tins several weeks before eating. Flavor improves with age.

Lebkuchen

Spicy cookies and cakes have been made in Northern Europe since the early days of trading with the Orient. Fragrant with cinnamon, cloves, cardamom, mace, nutmeg, coriander, and embellished with the peels of oranges, lemons, and citron, these delicacies became traditional holiday fare, taking on characteristics of particular countries as recipes were refined and handed down the generations. The honey and spices, natural preservatives, combine to make cookies that can be stored for months, and in fact mellow and improve in flavor and texture from the aging process. Although they are associated with winter and the holidays, all honey-spice cookies are tasty with a dish of fruit in any season; consider them for a regular spot on the pantry shelf. These Christmas cookies, in the German style, are the recipe of a dear friend who always makes them at Christmas and recalls that her mother always did, too.

2¾ cups flour
1 tsp. cinnamon
1 tsp. ground cloves
1 tsp. allspice
1 tsp. nutmeg, freshly grated
½ cup honey
½ cup molasses

¾ cup brown sugar
1 egg, beaten
1 Tbsp. lemon juice
grated rind of one lemon
⅓ cup citron, chopped, or candied orange peel
⅓ cup nuts, chopped

Glaze: ½ cup powdered sugar, 2 Tbsp. cornstarch, ½ tsp. vanilla or brandy, 1–3 Tbsp. hot water

Sift the flour with spices and set aside. Heat the honey, molasses, and brown sugar to a boil in a large, heavy saucepan; cool to lukewarm. Stir in the egg and lemon juice. Grate the lemon rind directly into the pan so no aromatic oils are lost. Stir in the flour in several additions, mixing thoroughly. Work in citron or orange peel and nuts. Cover and chill overnight. Preheat oven to 400° and lightly grease baking sheets. On a floured board roll the dough ¼″ thick, a small amount at a time; keep the remainder refrigerated. Cut into rectangles 1½″x2½″. Place one inch apart on the baking sheets to allow for spreading. Bake 10–12 minutes, until the edges have browned. Mix the glaze together, stirring powdered sugar, cornstarch, and vanilla with just enough hot water to make a smooth thick paste. Remove the cookies to a cooling rack and brush with glaze while hot, using a pastry brush. Cool thoroughly and store in airtight tins. Age several days before eating; will keep for months.

Baseler leckerli

Swiss holiday spice cookies, *leckerli* should be baked several weeks or even months before they are wanted. They become hard after they cool, and it takes weeks to develop a fine texture. A piece of bread or wedge of apple can be stored in the tin to hasten softening.

1 ¼ cups honey
⅓ cup kirsch
1 cup sugar
grated rind of one lemon
¼ cup chopped candied lemon peel, homemade preferred
¼ cup chopped candied orange peel, homemade preferred
1 cup grated almonds

4 cups flour
1 Tbsp. cinnamon
1 tsp. nutmeg
½ tsp. ground cloves
pinch salt
1 tsp. baking soda

Glaze: same as *lebkuchen*

Bring the honey to a boil in a large saucepan, watching carefully (like milk, it can bolt). Off the heat, stir in kirsch and sugar. Return to low heat and stir until sugar has melted. Let cool. Grate the lemon rind directly into the pan so no aromatic oils will be lost, and add fruit peels. Stir in almonds. Sift together the flour, spices, salt, and soda; stir in. Add flour as required to make a dough that will clear the sides of the pan. Cover and ripen in a cool place overnight, several days or a week. To roll out: preheat oven to 325°; butter baking sheets heavily and dust with flour. Roll dough ¼″ thick on a lightly floured surface and cut into rectangles. Place close together on baking pans and bake 20–25 minutes, until uniformly golden. Remove to cooling racks and brush with glaze while warm. Store in airtight tins and age several weeks before serving. They keep for months.

BULGARIAN HONEY COOKIES
Medeni kurabii

Freshly baked, these cookies have the quality of fine pastry; as they age they continue to be flavorful but they fall into the honey-soft syndrome. While these cookies are easily made, shaping them is a sticky business and you also need to pay careful attention when removing them from the baking sheets.

½ cup sweet butter	1 cup flour, *more if needed*
¼ cup honey	1 tsp. baking soda
3 Tbsp. sugar	large-crystal granulated
1 egg yolk	sugar

Preheat oven to 350°. Melt the butter in a small pan without browning. Pour into a small, deep bowl, leaving the milky residue in the saucepan. Let the butter cool, then stir in honey, sugar, and egg yolk. Sift the soda and flour together and add a few spoons at a time, mixing in each addition thoroughly. The batter should be just firm enough to hold a shape; add more flour if needed. Pinch off dough a teaspoon at a time, shape into a ball between your palms (it's sticky and perfect spheres are not essential), dip the ball in sugar, and place sugar-side-up on an ungreased baking sheet. Leave room for cookies to spread; it's easiest to bake a dozen at a time. Bake 10 minutes, until puffed and golden. Cool them briefly on the baking sheet to make them less fragile, and then remove carefully with a metal spatula to cooling racks. Eat when cool or store in airtight tins. Makes 24 cookies.

ITALIAN PINE NUT COOKIES *Pignoli*

Pine nuts are native only to the Western part of the United States, but they are plentiful in Italy, southern France, and the Middle East, where they are used in sweets and pilafs and meat dishes. *Pignoli* are delicate in flavor, nice with fruit or ice cream after a hearty pasta meal.

½ cup butter	1 cup flour
2 Tbsp. honey	2 tsp. brandy
1 Tbsp. sugar	½ cup pine nuts

Preheat oven to 375°. Lightly grease baking sheets. Cream the butter, incorporating sugar and honey. Mix in flour and brandy, then pine nuts. Shape by the teaspoonful into small balls with the palms of your hands. Place on baking sheets one inch apart; they will spread slightly but remain uniformly round because of the shaping method. Bake 10 minutes, until pale gold. Cool on racks.

POLISH CHRISTMAS TREE COOKIES *Ciastka miodowe*

½ cup sweet butter	½ tsp. ground cloves
1 cup sugar	¼ tsp. nutmeg, freshly grated
1 cup honey	
2 Tbsp. cream	grated rind of one lemon
1 Tbsp. cinnamon	3½–4 cups flour, *more if needed*
1½ tsp. ginger	

Preheat oven to 350°. Grease and flour baking sheets. Cream the butter with the sugar until light and fluffy. Add the honey, cream, spices, and blend thoroughly. Grate the lemon rind directly into the bowl so no aromatic oils are lost. Sift the flour and add it gradually to the butter mixture, beating well after each addition, until the dough is stiff enough to roll. Chill briefly. Roll out ⅛" thick on a floured surface and cut into desired shapes; dough may be somewhat sticky. Transfer the cookies carefully to the baking sheets and bake 10 minutes, or until just beginning to brown around the edges. Cool on a rack. Store in an airtight jar. To make cookies sturdy enough to hang on the Christmas tree, add up to ½ cup additional flour to make a stiffer dough. Before baking, make a small hole in each cookie with the tip of a paring knife. When cool, ice the cookies with white icing and candies, string yarn through the holes, and tie on tree branches.

HONEY-DIPPED GREEK NUT COOKIES
Finikia

2 cups flour	¼ cup orange juice
½ tsp. salt	1 tsp. vanilla
¾ tsp. baking powder	1 cup Basic Honey Syrup
½ cup sweet butter	(see recipe)
6 Tbsp. powdered sugar	2 cups walnuts, very
¼ cup bland oil	finely chopped
2 Tbsp. egg, *beat an egg and measure 2 Tbsp.*	

Preheat oven to 350°. Lightly grease two large baking sheets. Sift together the flour, salt, and baking powder; set aside. Cream together the butter and sugar; incorporate the oil a little at a time, then the egg, orange juice, and vanilla. To avoid separation, add in very small amounts, mixing well in between. If the mixture appears curdled, it will recombine when the flour is added. Add the flour half a cup at a time, mixing well. With your hands shape small pieces of the dough into ovals about 2″ long; add a little flour if needed to make dough manageable. Place an inch apart on baking sheets and bake 20 minutes, until they are just beginning to color. Cool on racks. Warm the syrup and spread the walnuts on a shallow dish such as a pie plate. Dip each cookie in the syrup and then roll in the nuts. Return to the rack to dry before serving. Store loosely covered; they keep several days. Makes 30 cookies.

LITHUANIAN SPICE COOKIES *Grybai*

Because of their unusual presentation in the shape of fat forest mushrooms, painted with glaze, these Lithuanian cookies make a whimsical addition to a holiday tray. The balance of spices is particularly pleasing. Like all honey cookies, these keep well, so the time-consuming handiwork can be planned for a day well ahead of the time they are wanted.

4 cups flour	½ tsp. cardamom
1½ tsp. baking soda	grated rind of one orange
1 tsp. cinnamon	1 cup honey
½ tsp. ground cloves	¼ cup butter
½ tsp. ginger	⅜ cup sugar
½ tsp. nutmeg, freshly grated	¼ cup sour cream

Icing: 1½ cups powdered sugar, 4 tsp. cold water, 4 tsp. lemon juice, 1 Tbsp. cocoa

Sift together the flour, soda, and spices. Grate the orange rind directly into the bowl so no aromatic oils are lost, and set aside. Heat the honey to a boil and cool to lukewarm. Cream the butter and sugar together in a large mixing bowl until light and fluffy. Add the sour cream and honey, blending well. Add the flour mixture in small amounts, mixing thoroughly between additions. Shape the dough into a ball, cover, and refrigerate at least an hour. Preheat the oven to 350°. Grease baking sheets lightly. Divide the dough in two parts, one slightly larger than the other. From the larger piece, pull off about 30 pieces of dough and shape in your palms to balls a generous 1″ in diameter; these are the mushroom caps. There is no need for them to be uniform in size or shape. From the smaller ball of dough make the same number of small cylinders; these will be the stems. Place on baking sheets, allowing 1″ between cookies for spreading. Bake 10 minutes; remove to racks for cooling. Mix together powdered sugar, water, and lemon juice to make a smooth, opaque icing. Line up the cylinder stems and place a dot of icing at the top of each. Set a cap in position on top, tilted like a sombrero. Let them dry in position. Then paint the stem portion with the white glaze; let dry. Add cocoa to make a dark icing and brush on the mushroom caps. Serve at once or store tightly covered.

CANADIAN NUT WAFERS

England since colonial times has made brandy snaps—crisp, lacy wafers folded or rolled into a cone, filled with whipped cream, and presented as a technical problem to diners: you can either shatter the whole with a blow from your fork and scoop up pieces swathed in cream, or you continuously bite off pieces, keeping a saucer hovering at your chin. This Canadian derivation from the original is practically a nut brittle, a nice contrast to butter cookies in an assortment.

1 cup flour	½ cup less 1 Tbsp. sugar
¼ tsp. nutmeg, freshly grated	1 scant cup honey
¼ tsp. cinnamon	1 egg
¼ tsp. mace	½ cup chopped almonds
½ cup butter	

Preheat oven to 300°. Lightly grease baking sheets. Sift together the flour and spices and set aside. Cream the butter with the sugar and beat in the egg; add honey, stirring until well mixed. Stir in the flour, one half at a time, blending well. Add nuts. Drop by the teaspoonful onto baking sheets, allowing space for prodigious spreading; six to a sheet is a comfortable quantity. Bake about 12 minutes, until uniformly light brown. Avoid scorching, as they are flavored by overbaking. Leave the cookies on the pan a moment, then remove carefully with a metal spatula and drape over a rolling pin or the edge of a colander. If they become too cold to be pliable, return to the oven a moment to soften. They become crisp when cooled. If desired, these cookies can be rolled into cornucopias and filled with brandy-flavored whipped cream. Humidity is their downfall. Store tightly covered, or bake just before serving, allowing time for cooling.

CARDAMOM CAKE

3 cups cake flour	½ cup butter
3 tsp. baking powder	¾ cup sugar
1 tsp. cardamom	3 eggs
¾ tsp. salt	1 cup minus 3 Tbsp. milk
¾ cup honey	

Preheat oven to 350°. Grease a 9x13 cake pan, line the bottom with waxed paper cut to fit, and grease the paper. Sift together three times the flour, baking powder, cardamom, and salt, and set aside. In a large bowl cream the butter, then add honey and beat until fluffy and smooth. Add sugar, beating until it is well incorporated. Add the eggs one at a time, beating well after each addition. Add the dry ingredients alternately with the milk, beginning and ending with dry ingredients. Beat thoroughly between additions. Pour the batter into the prepared pan and bake 40–45 minutes, until a cake tester inserted at the center comes out clean. Cool in pan for 10 minutes, then turn out onto a rack, peel off the waxed paper, and allow to cool completely. Cut in squares to serve.

VARIATION: Bake the cake in two 9″ layer cake pans, similarly prepared; they will be done in 20–25 minutes. Frost if desired with caramel or fresh orange icing.

CHRISTMAS GINGERBREAD LOAF

½ cup honey
½ tsp. ginger
½ tsp. cinnamon
½ tsp. ground cloves
1 ¼ cup flour
½ tsp. baking powder
½ tsp. baking soda
¼ tsp. salt
¼ cup butter
¼ cup brown sugar
grated rind of half
    a lemon

1 small egg
½ cup buttermilk
1 cup Honey Lemon
    Filling (recipe follows)
2 cups cream, whipped
    and sweetened
candied lemon peel,
    for garnish, homemade
    preferred

Preheat oven to 350°. Grease a 9″ square pan. In a small saucepan, combine honey and spices, bring to a boil, remove from the heat and cool. Sift the flour with baking powder, soda, and salt and set aside. Cream the butter and brown sugar until light and fluffy. Add the cooled honey-spice mixture and blend thoroughly. Grate the lemon rind directly into the bowl and add the egg, mixing until well blended. Add the flour and buttermilk alternately, beating well after each addition. Pour into the prepared pan and bake 30–35 minutes, until a cake tester comes out clean. Cool in the pan 10 minutes, then turn out on a rack to cool completely. Make Honey Lemon Filling. Cut the cooled cake in half and layer the halves with the filling. Frost the entire loaf with the sweetened whipped cream. Decorate the top with flowerettes of candied lemon peel. Chill for two hours before serving.

Honey Lemon Filling

¼ cup honey
1½ Tbsp. potato starch
 flour
⅛ tsp. salt
⅓ cup water

1 egg yolk
½ Tbsp. butter
 grated rind of two lemons
5 Tbsp. lemon juice

In a small saucepan, combine the honey, potato starch flour, and salt. Stir in the water gradually. Bring to a boil, stirring constantly, and boil one minute. Remove from heat and stir half of the mixture into the egg yolk, slightly beaten. Blend this mixture into the remaining syrup in the saucepan and boil one minute more. Off heat, add butter and lemon rind and stir in the lemon juice gradually. Cool. Store in a covered jar in the refrigerator if not used immediately.

CHOCOLATE HONEY CUPCAKES

1 cup cake flour
¼ tsp. salt
¼ tsp. baking soda
¾ tsp. baking powder
3 Tbsp. honey
⅓ cup milk
2 Tbsp. water

2 oz. German's sweet
 chocolate
¼ cup butter
½ cup honey
1 egg
½ tsp. vanilla

Preheat oven to 375°. Grease and flour a cupcake pan or popover pan, or line with paper cups. Sift together the flour, salt, baking powder, and soda. Set aside. In a small, heavy saucepan combine the 3 Tbsp. honey, milk, water, and chocolate. Stir over very low heat until the chocolate is melted and the mixture well blended. Cool. Cream the butter until fluffy; add the ½ cup honey in a thin stream, beating constantly. When the mixture is light and smooth, add the egg and vanilla, blending well. Alternately add the dry ingredients and the chocolate mixture, beginning and ending with the dry ingredients. Mix just until smooth. Fill the pan ⅔ full and bake 18–20 minutes until rounded and a cake tester in the center comes out clean. Turn out on a rack to cool. Frost the tops by swirling the cakes in a bowl of fresh orange icing. Makes 8 medium cupcakes.

WHOLE WHEAT LEMON YOGURT LOAF

½ cup butter	grated rind of one lemon
½ cup sugar	1½ cups flour
¼ cup honey	1½ cups whole wheat
3 eggs, separated	pastry flour
½ cup plain yogurt	2 tsp. baking powder
½ Tbsp. lemon juice	pinch salt

Preheat oven to 350°. Butter an 8x4 baking pan. Cream together the butter, honey, and ¼ cup of sugar. Beat in the three egg yolks. Grate the lemon rind directly into the bowl so no aromatic oils are lost, and add the yogurt and lemon juice. Sift together the flours, baking powder, and salt; mix into the creamed ingredients in two additions. Beat the reserved egg whites with the remaining ¼ cup sugar until glossy and fold in gently. Pour into prepared pan. Bake one hour, or until browned; reduce heat if browning too rapidly. Cake is done when a tester in the center comes out clean. Cool in the pan, then remove and wrap well to store; will keep two or three days.

UKRAINIAN HONEY CAKE *Medivnyk*

Clear orange flavor distinguishes this honey cake, which is otherwise very similar to the cakes made in Holland and Germany; fruits may be omitted for a simpler cake.

2 Tbsp. butter	¼ tsp. salt
½ cup sugar	¼ cup cold coffee
2 egg yolks	¼ cup orange juice
½ cup honey	grated rind of two oranges
1½ cups flour	½ tsp. vanilla
½ tsp. baking soda	½ cup walnuts, chopped
½ tsp. baking powder	½ cup golden raisins
¼ tsp. cinnamon	½ cup chopped dates
¼ tsp. allspice	2 egg whites

Preheat oven to 350°. Butter a 9x5 loaf pan heavily. Cream the butter and sugar; add egg yolks and beat in honey in a thin stream. Into a large mixing bowl sift the flour with soda, baking powder, spices, and salt. Grate the orange rind directly into the bowl. Stir in one third of the dry ingredients, then coffee, an additional third dry ingredients, the orange juice, and the last of the dry ingredients. Stir in vanilla and walnuts. Beat the egg whites until siff but not dry; fold in gently. The batter is heavy and this requires care. Push into the buttered pan and bake about one hour, until a tester comes out clean. Cool in pan a few minutes before turning out to cool on a rack. Wrap well and age a day before serving. Keeps several weeks, well wrapped.

ESTONIAN HONEY CAKE *Mee kook*

A particularly moist and delicate honey cake decorated with whole blanched almonds.

1 cup dark honey, such as Buckwheat

1½ tsp. cinnamon

½ tsp. nutmeg, freshly grated

½ tsp. cardamom

¼ tsp. ginger

¼ tsp. ground cloves

2½ cups flour

2 tsp. baking soda

pinch of salt

½ cup butter

1 cup sugar

6 eggs, separated

grated rind of one lemon

½ cup milk

Grease and flour a 9 inch tube pan or 10 inch spring form pan. Arrange whole blanched almonds on the bottom of the pan to form a decorative pattern. Preheat oven to 375°. In a small heavy saucepan combine the honey and spices; bring to a boil, then remove from heat and allow to cool. Sift the flour once, then resift with the baking soda and salt and set aside. In a large bowl, cream the butter and sugar until the sugar is well incorporated and the mixture is light and fluffy. Beat the room temperature egg whites until stiff but not dry, using a wire whip or electric mixer. To assemble the cake, add the reserved egg yolks to the creamed butter-sugar mixture and beat until smooth and well blended. Then stir in the cooled spiced honey and the lemon rind. Add the flour to the batter alternately with the milk, beginning and ending with the flour, beating well between additions. Finally, carefully fold the beaten whites into the batter, using a large rubber spatula. Incorporate as well as possible without deflating them. Pour into prepared pan and bake for 40 minutes in the preheated oven. Reduce heat to 325° and bake 20 minutes more, or until a cake tester comes out clean. Cool for at least ten minutes on a wire rack. Remove from pan and allow to cool completely. Wrap it carefully (it's soft and can be dented by a foil wrap applied too firmly) and store in the pantry for two days before cutting. The cake improves with age.

JEWISH HOLIDAY HONEY CAKE

1 ¾ cup sifted flour
⅛ tsp. salt
¾ tsp. baking powder
½ tsp. baking soda
¼ tsp. cinnamon
¼ tsp. ginger
⅛ tsp. nutmeg, freshly grated

⅛ tsp. ground cloves
2 eggs
6 Tbsp. sugar
2 Tbsp. bland oil
1 cup honey
¼ cup cold coffee
¾ cup chopped nuts

Preheat oven to 325°. Grease a 9x5 inch loaf pan. Sift the flour, salt, baking powder, baking soda, and spices together and set aside. Beat the eggs; then add the sugar gradually, beating until the mixture is thick and lemon-colored. Combine the oil, honey, and coffee in a large measuring cup; pour into the egg mixture and blend well. Add the flour-spice mixture and the nuts, stirring until all ingredients are moistened and the batter is smooth. Turn into the pan and bake 40–50 minutes, until nicely browned and a cake tester comes out clean. Cool in the pan ten minutes before turning out onto a rack to cool completely. Wrap in foil to store.

Lekach

A very satisfactory cake, distinguished by the flavor of fresh candied citrus peel and a hint of brandy.

3½ cups flour
1 tsp. baking soda
1½ tsp. baking powder
½ tsp. ground cardamom
½ tsp. allspice
½ tsp. cinnamon
½ cup sliced almonds
½ cup raisins
½ cup chopped candied orange
   peel or lemon peel or a
   combination of both

4 eggs
1 cup sugar
1 cup honey
½ cup cold coffee
2 Tbsp. bland oil
2 Tbsp. brandy or cognac

Grease a 10x15 pan at least 2″ deep: a small roasting pan does nicely. Line with waxed paper cut to fit the pan and grease the paper. Preheat oven to 300°. Sift together the flour, baking soda, baking powder, and spices. Stir in the nuts, raisins, and candied peels and set aside. In a medium bowl, beat the eggs lightly with a wire whip. Still beating, add the sugar gradually and beat until the mixture is light and fluffy. Measure the honey, coffee, and oil into a large measuring cup and combine thoroughly. Add this mixture to the eggs and sugar and blend well. Next add the dry ingredients and the brandy, stirring until the batter is smooth. Pour into the prepared pan and bake one hour. Cool in the pan for ten minutes before inverting onto a wire rack. Peel off the waxed paper and allow the cake to cool completely. Although this cake may be eaten immediately while still warm, once cooled it is best aged at least a week, wrapped in aluminum foil. Cut into squares or diamonds to serve, and sprinkle with powdered sugar.

FRENCH SPICE LOAF *Pain d'epice*

One of the few French pastries using honey, *pain d'epice* has a special place in household ritual as a teatime sweet. It is buttered and served with marmalade. At a wonderful tea in Versailles it was spread with sour cream and placed on a *biscotte*, a packaged toast like our rusk. This snack, with its fascinating contrast of textures, did very nicely to tide one over till dinner. Excellent *pain d'epice* is made commercially, and it is considered a regional specialty of Dijon. Many Americans who think they don't like anise will find this cake a palatable introduction to the spice; or cinnamon, nutmeg, mace, ginger can be substituted to create a flavor balance that is individually pleasing.

1 cup dark honey
1 cup sugar
3 tsp. baking soda
1 cup hot water
2 tsp. anise seeds
grated rind of one orange
    or ¼ cup candied
    orange peel, chopped

pinch salt
½ tsp. dry mustard
2¾ cups flour
¾ cup rye flour

Combine honey, sugar, and soda in a large bowl. Pour the hot water over them and stir. Crush the anise seeds in a mortar and pestle and add. Grate the orange rind directly into the bowl, so no aromatic oils will be lost. Add salt and mustard, and other spices if desired. Stir in flour gradually, mixing well. Set this batter aside for several days or a week in a cool place (not the refrigerator). The cake can be baked at once, but flavor improves with aging and a lovely silken texture develops in the batter. Preheat oven to 350°. Butter heavily two small loaf pans. Bake one hour. Brush the surface of the loaf with hot milk when it comes from the oven. Cool in the pan 10 minutes, then turn onto racks to complete cooling. Well wrapped, this keeps for weeks.

New England HONEY PUMPKIN PIE

pastry for a one-crust
  9″ pie
6 Tbsp. honey
1 cup light cream
2 cups unsweetened
  pumpkin puree
4 eggs, beaten

1 tsp. cinnamon
½ tsp. ginger
½ tsp. mace
½ tsp. ground cloves
¾ tsp. salt

Preheat oven to 450°. Stir the honey into the light cream in a thin stream, then stir into the pumpkin puree. Add the eggs, which have been beaten together, and the seasonings. Pour into the prepared pie shell. Bake at 450° for 10 minutes, then reduce temperature to 325° and bake until filling is set, about 40 minutes. Serve with a wedge of New Hampshire cheddar cheese or with spiced whipped cream.

WEST COAST RAISIN PIE

pastry for a two-crust
  9″ pie
2 cups raisins
grated rind of one
  orange
1 cup orange juice
¼ cup lemon juice

5 Tbsp. honey, orange
  blossom preferred
pinch salt
4 Tbsp. potato starch
  flour
¾ cup cold water
2 Tbsp. butter

Place in a medium saucepan the raisins, orange and lemon juices, honey, and salt; grate the orange rind directly into the pan. Dissolve the potato starch flour in the water and add to the raisin mixture. Cook, stirring constantly, over medium heat until thick and smooth. Stir in the butter. Cool. Preheat oven to 425°. Line a 9″ pie plate with pastry and fill with the cooled raisin mixture. Roll out a cover, cut vents, and fit in place, sealing well. Bake until golden brown, 30–40 minutes.

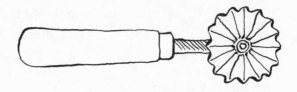

DEEP SOUTH SWEET POTATO PIE

pastry for a one-crust 9″ pie	pinch salt
4 eggs	1 tsp. vanilla
6 Tbsp. honey	1½ cups mashed cooked yams
⅔ cup cream	⅓ cup cream
⅓ cup orange juice	nutmeg, freshly grated

Preheat oven to 450°. Line a pie plate with the pastry, building up a fluted edge. Chill while mixing the filling. Beat eggs thoroughly; stir in honey, cream, orange juice, salt, vanilla; add to the puree yams and stir until well mixed. Pour into the prepared crust and bake at 450° for 10 minutes; reduce heat to 350° and bake 30 minutes more, or until only the center jiggles when the pan is gently shaken. Cool. Whip the ⅓ cup cream and flavor with freshly grated nutmeg. Spread on top of the pie and serve. One half of the filling recipe is sufficient for an 8″ tart; bake in the same way. Makes 6 dessert servings.

MOM'S PIE CRUST

- 2 cups flour
- 1 tsp. salt
- ⅞ cup shortening: half butter, half lard
- 3-4 Tbsp. ice water

Measure the flour into a large mixing bowl. Sprinkle the salt over it and chunk the butter and lard into the bowl. Cut in with a pastry blender until it resembles a fine meal. Sprinkle a minimum amount of ice water over the surface and rub the dough together with your fingertips until it barely clings together in a ball, adding more water as needed. Turn out on a piece of waxed paper, shaking any excess flour or loose particles from the bowl on top; wrap tightly and chill two hours or overnight before rolling out. Roll on a lightly floured board, shaping as desired. Makes a two-crust 9″ pie.

When I set out the ingredients for this dough, I measure ¼ cup water and put an ice cube in the cup. It is well chilled when added to the dough, and the object here as with all fat-cut-into-flour formulas is to avoid coating the flour with soft fat.

PEACH TART, NOUGAT TOPPING

- Sweet Tart Pastry for 9″ pan
- 2½ cup sliced peaches
- 3 Tbsp. cream
- 3 Tbsp. butter
- 3 Tbsp. honey
- 3 Tbsp. sliced unblanched almonds

Line the tart pan with Sweet Tart Pastry, chill and prebake according to recipe instructions. Cool while preparing the filling. Place the cream, butter, and honey in a medium saucepan and boil over medium heat, watching carefully, until light brown. Stir in the nuts and set aside. Peel and slice the peaches and arrange in the tart shell. Strew about a third of the fruit in the bottom of the shell and arrange the rest in neat concentric circles on top. Spoon the nougat topping over the fruit. Bake at 375° until fruit is tender and juices bubble, 35–45 minutes. Cool.

VARIATION: The pastry used for Ricotta Tart is excellent with peaches, nectarines, and apricots; any of them may be substituted in this recipe. Apricots should be halved and placed cut side down very close together; they need not be peeled. Nectarines also need not be peeled unless you object to the slightly shrivelled skins that result from baking.

SPICED APPLE TART

One half recipe Walnut Tart Pastry (see below)
2 cups tart green apples, peeled and sliced
¼ cup honey
1 Tbsp. butter
vanilla, a few drops
cardamom

Line an 8″ tart pan with removable bottom with the pastry, rolling out the ample scraps into an 8x6 rectangle ¼″ thick. Cut into 8 strips to make a lattice top. Chill one hour. Preheat oven to 375°. Spread the sliced apples in the chilled shell and drizzle with honey, dot with butter, sprinkle with vanilla. Crush the dark seeds from whole cardamom pods in a mortar and pestle to make ⅛ tsp. finely ground spice, and dust this over the apples. Weave the pastry strips in a lattice pattern over the top, pressing the ends firmly to the edge of the shell. Bake 35–45 minutes, until apples are tender and pastry is golden. Cool on a rack.

Walnut Tart Pastry: Substitute ½ cup grated walnuts for ½ cup flour in the Sweet Tart Pastry; proceed as usual.

BERRIES & CHEESE TART

Sweet Tart Pastry
   for 9″ pan
4 oz. cream cheese
¼ cup whipping cream,
   approximately
1 tsp. honey

¼ tsp. vanilla
1 pint blueberries
2 Tbsp. light honey
lemon juice as needed

Line the tart pan with pastry, chill, and prebake as directed. Cool while preparing the filling. Wash the blueberries and sort through carefully, removing any stems or inferior berries. Place one quarter of the berries in a small saucepan with 2 Tbsp. honey and cook over medium heat until a fairly thick jam. Off heat, add lemon juice to taste; large cultivated berries tend to be quite sweet and may require a tablespoon; tiny sour berries may need no additional tartness. Mix the warm jam through the uncooked berries and cool. Place the cream cheese in a small deep mixing bowl and begin whipping it, adding a thin stream of cream. When it has reached a nice spreading consistency, add honey to taste and vanilla; use cream only as needed. Shortly before serving, spread the cheese in the cooled pastry crust and top with berries.

VARIATION: Top the cream cheese mixture in the shell with neat rows of strawberries, hulled and placed stem side down. Boil 3 Tbsp. currant jelly in a small pan until thickened and brush carefully over the berries to glaze them. The whipped cream cheese is delicious served with many fruits for dessert. A little more cream can be used and the soft mixture spooned over bowls of strawberries.

SWEET TART PASTRY

2⅔ cups flour
¼ cup sugar
   pinch salt
   grated rind of one lemon
1 cup cold butter
2 egg yolks

Place the flour in a medium mixing bowl and sprinkle sugar and salt over it. Grate the lemon directly into the bowl so no aromatic oils are lost. With a knife cut the butter into small pieces, dropping them into the flour. Using your fingertips, work the butter and flour together until it resembles meal; do not let it get pasty. Add the egg yolks, mix, and gather into a ball. Divide into portions for desired use and press the pastry into the baking pans. This amount will fill two 9″ tart pans. Any bits left over can be used to fill tiny tart pans; accumulate in the freezer until you have enough to serve. Chill the pastry-lined pans 30 minutes to an hour, or freeze until wanted. If they are to be filled and baked, prebake at 450° 15 minutes, until the shine has disappeared but before they are brown. Cool on a rack. Fill and bake according to filling directions. If tarts will have an uncooked filling such as fresh berries, bake at 375° 35–45 minutes until golden brown. Cool on a rack. Pastry may be stored in the refrigerator, well wrapped, for several days.

GREEK HONEY PIE *Melopeta*

Pastry

1½ cups flour
¼ tsp. salt
½ cup butter
1 egg, beaten

Blend the flour and salt. Chunk the butter into the bowl, then cut it into the flour with a pastry blender until you have pea-size particles. Add the egg and stir with a fork. Work together with your fingertips until well blended. Wrap and chill at least one hour. Roll the dough out between sheets of waxed paper until ⅛" thick. Every few strokes, peel off the top layer and replace, in order to help the dough spread out evenly. Press the dough into an 8" pie plate, fluting the edge to form a high rim. Chill 30 minutes. Preheat oven to 425° Prebake the chilled shell 10 minutes. Cool while preparing the filling. Reduce oven heat to 325°.

Filling

1½ pounds ricotta cheese
6–8 Tbsp. honey
¼ tsp. cinnamon
5 eggs

Blend together the cheese, honey, and cinnamon, using 8 Tbsp. honey if a sweeter pie is wanted. Beat in the eggs one at a time. Pour the filling into the pie shell and bake 50 minutes, or until a knife inserted in the center comes out clean. Cool on a wire rack and chill. Serve cold. Only slightly sweet, this pastry can be a lunch or picnic main dish as well as dessert.

ITALIAN RICOTTA TART

Pastries like this of cheese sweetened with honey have been made since Roman times. The effect of the liqueurs for flavoring seems similar in kind to the ancient use of perfumes.

Pastry

2 cups flour	1 egg yolk
3 Tbsp. sugar	2 Tbsp. dry sherry
½ tsp. salt	
½ cup plus 2 Tbsp. cold butter	

Sift the flour, sugar, and salt together into a mixing bowl. Cut the butter in large flakes into the flour. Add the egg yolk and mix together with the fingertips until the fat is well coated by flour, then sprinkle in sherry as needed so the dough adheres in a ball. Wrap in waxed paper and refrigerate about an hour so it is easier to handle. Roll out less than ¼" thick and fit into a 9" tart pan with removable bottom; avoid stretching the pastry so it will not shrink. Build a small edge. Cut 8 to 10 strips ½" wide from a rectangle rolled out of the ample trimmings; these will be used for a lattice top. Chill shell while mixing the filling. Preheat oven to 375°.

Filling

12 oz. ricotta cheese	2 Tbsp. sliced almonds
2 Tbsp. honey	2 Tbsp. pine nuts
2 eggs	1 Tbsp. kirsch
2 Tbsp. candied orange peel, chopped, homemade preferred	1 Tbsp. Grand Marnier

Sieve the ricotta into a mixing bowl. Add the honey, eggs, fruit peel, nuts, and liqueurs, mixing until smooth. Pour into the prepared shell and weave a lattice top with the strips of dough. Bake 45 minutes, until puffed and golden. Serve barely warm or cooled, dusted with powdered sugar.

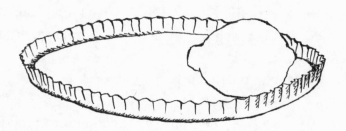

SWISS WALNUT TART *Engadiner nusstorte*

A famous Swiss specialty, this walnut praline tart is elegant and fantastically rich; serve it in small wedges.

Pastry

3 cups flour	1 egg
3 Tbsp. sugar	grated rind of
pinch salt	two lemons
1 cup butter, cold	1 Tbsp. rum

Place the flour in a large mixing bowl and mix the sugar and salt through it. Cut the butter into large flakes, letting them drop into the flour. With your fingertips work the cold butter and flour together to make a coarse meal. Break the egg into a large measuring cup, add the rum. Grate the lemons directly into the bowl of dough, add the egg mixture, and toss all together with a fork until well combined; with your hands, work together into a firm ball. Chill at least two hours before rolling out. On a lightly floured surface roll ¾ of the dough ⅛″ thick; line a 9″ springform with the pastry, fitting it in without stretching so that it will not shrink. Chill the pastry-lined pan and reserved dough while preparing filling. Preheat oven to 350°.

Filling

   1   cup heavy cream
1 ¼   cups sugar
   3   Tbsp. honey
   2   Tbsp. kirsch
   3   cups walnuts, broken

Glaze: 1 egg yolk, 2 Tbsp. cream

Scald the cream and set aside. Caramelize the sugar in a large dry skillet, stirring to keep uniform browning. When it is caramel-color, add the warm cream slowly, stirring constantly. When the mixture is smooth and evenly mixed, remove from heat and add remaining ingredients. Pour into the prepared pan. Roll out the remaining dough ⅛″ thick and cut into eight or ten strips about 10″ long. Use them to weave a lattice topping. Press edges firmly to the edge of the tart shell. Mix together the egg yolk and cream; brush all surfaces with this glaze. Bake 40–45 minutes, until golden brown. Cool in pan.

Baklava

To many people *Baklava* is the favorite honey sweet: dozens of layers of filo, the whisper-thin pastry sheets, filled with butter and almonds and drenched in a spicy honey syrup. Packaged frozen filo is available in many supermarkets and in Greek and Mediterranean groceries; follow package directions for handling.

1½ cups almonds, finely chopped
½ pound filo pastry sheets
½ cup melted sweet butter
  Basic Honey Syrup, about one cup, *see recipe*

Spread the finely chopped almonds on a jelly roll pan and toast at 325° for 15 minutes, until golden brown. Transfer to a large plate and set aside. Reset oven to 350° Unroll the filo dough and place an 8″ round cake pan on a stack of sheets. Using the pan as a pattern, cut all around with a sharp knife to make pastry circles. Repeat the process to make another stack. On the remaining border of filo, cut a stack of semi-circles large enough to cover the bottom of the pan, overlapped. Butter the cake pan. Place one circle of dough on the bottom of the pan and brush with melted butter; repeat for six layers. Spread ¼ cup almonds over this pastry base. Cover with a circle of dough, brush with butter and sprinkle with a scant tablespoon of almonds; repeat for 15 layers. Once or twice as the stack grows, press it together with your hand. Finish with six layers of filo only, brushing each with butter. Score ½″ deep with the tip of a sharp knife into 16 triangular pieces. Bake for 45 minutes, until a rich golden brown. While still hot, pour the cooled honey syrup over the pastry. Slice through the remaining layers of filo and let cool in pan several hours before serving.

GREEK WALNUT CAKE *Karidopeta*

½ cup sifted flour
½ cup farina (regular Cream of Wheat)
½ cup finely chopped walnuts
1½ tsp. baking powder
½ tsp. cinnamon

grated rind of half an orange
½ cup butter
½ cup sugar
3 eggs
Basic Honey Syrup, about ¾ cup, *see recipe*

Preheat oven to 350°. Grease an 8″ square pan. In a small bowl combine the flour, farina, nuts, baking powder, and cinnamon; grate the orange rind directly into the bowl so no aromatic oils are lost. Set aside. In a large bowl, cream the butter with sugar until light and fluffy. Add the eggs one at a time, beating constantly. Add the dry ingredients in two parts and mix thoroughly. Pour into pan and bake for 30 minutes. Remove and place on a rack. Pour about ¾ cup cooled Basic Honey Syrup over the warm cake, being careful to soak every part of it. Cool. Cut into squares or diamonds to serve. This cake may be doubled and baked in a 9x13 pan, using twice as much syrup. Since it is served directly from the pan it is ideal for a picnic.

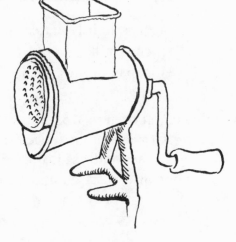

Kadaife

1 cup walnuts or almonds,
  finely chopped
1 cup sweet butter
⅓ cup sugar
1 egg
¾ tsp. cinnamon

8 large shredded wheat
  biscuits
milk for soaking
¼ cup melted butter
Basic Honey Syrup, about
  ¾ cup, *see recipe*

Preheat oven to 375°. Butter an 8″ square pan. Cream together the nuts, butter, sugar, egg, and cinnamon to make a thick paste. Saturate four shredded wheat biscuits in milk, drain slightly, and place in the pan. Spread the nut filling over each biscuit in an even layer. Dip the remaining four biscuits in milk and place on top. Pour the melted butter evenly over the pastries. Bake 30 minutes, until the top is a crisp, golden brown. Heat Basic Honey Syrup and pour over the hot pastry to saturate. Cool in pan; cut each biscuit mound into thirds to serve. Especially delicious when barely warm and still crisp on top.

HONEY CUSTARD

4 eggs, lightly beaten
2½ cups milk
⅓ cup honey, warmed
  slightly

¼ tsp. salt
½ tsp. vanilla
nutmeg, freshly grated

Preheat oven to 325°. Butter 8 custard cups and prepare a pan of hot water an inch deep to hold them. To the beaten eggs add honey, milk, salt, and vanilla. Mix thoroughly. Strain and pour into custard cups. Grate nutmeg onto the surface of each. Place in the hot water bath and bake 40 minutes, or until the center barely jiggles. Remove and cool slightly before serving, or chill.

PUMPKIN CUSTARD

⅔ cup cooked, mashed pumpkin
1½ cups milk
2 Tbsp. light honey
grating of nutmeg
2 eggs

Preheat oven to 325°. Butter 6 custard cups and prepare a pan of hot water an inch deep to hold them. Beat the eggs to mix thoroughly; add the other ingredients, blending until smooth. These can be whirled in a blender to mix. Divide among the custard cups; place in hot water bath and bake 30 minutes, or until only the center jiggles. Delicate and tasty at room temperature, or they may be served chilled.

BROWN RICE PUDDING

1½ cups cooked brown rice
½ cup water
1 cup milk
1 Tbsp. butter
½ cup chopped dried
apricots

2 eggs
5 Tbsp. honey
¼ tsp. salt
½ tsp. vanilla

Place the cooked rice in a saucepan, add the ½ cup water, and cook over medium heat until most of the water is absorbed.

Add the milk and cook a few minutes longer; remove from heat and stir in the butter and apricots. In a small bowl beat the 2 eggs with the honey, salt, and vanilla. Stir into the rice. Pour into a greased 1½ quart baking dish (a souffle dish is nice) and set into a pan of hot water. Place in a 325° oven and bake about 45 minutes, until only the center jiggles when the dish is gently moved. Good warm or cold. 6–8 servings.

STEAMED CRANBERRY PUDDING

1½ cups flour	⅓ cup hot water
½ tsp. salt	¼ tsp. ginger
1 tsp. baking soda	grated rind of
½ tsp. baking powder	one orange
2 cups cranberries	¼ cup almonds, chopped
⅔ cup honey	

Grease well a 1½ quart pudding basin, mold, or small bowl. Sift the dry ingredients and stir in the cranberries, which have been picked through to discard any soft ones. Dilute the honey with the hot water and add the liquid to the dry ingredients, beating to make a smooth batter. Grate the orange rind directly into the bowl and add ginger and nuts. Stir well. Pour into the prepared mold and cover tightly; use aluminum foil if there is no cover, and tie it firmly in place. The mold should be no more than ⅔ full, to allow for expansion. Place on a rack in a deep kettle and pour in hot water halfway up the sides of the mold. Cover the kettle, bring to a boil, then reduce heat to maintain a simmer for two hours while the pudding steams. Remove from pan and cool in the mold a few minutes before turning out on a serving plate. Serve hot in wedges, with Honeyed Brandy Butter or Honey Lemon Sauce.

STEAMED BLUEBERRY PUDDING

1 cup blueberries
2 cups flour
4 tsp. baking powder
½ tsp. salt

2 Tbsp. sugar
¼ cup honey
¾ cup milk
2 Tbsp. melted butter

Butter well a 1½ quart pudding mold, pudding basin, or small bowl. Set a kettle of water to boil, and choose a pot that will comfortably hold the mold. Sift the flour, baking powder, salt, and sugar into a bowl. Measure one cup blueberries that have been washed and pick over to remove stems and any wrinkled berries. Sprinkle a few spoons of the dry ingredients over the berries and shake through; they tend to sink less in the batter if coated with flour. Melt the 2 Tbsp. butter in a suacepan; remove from the heat and sitr in honey and milk. Add to the dry ingredients, then gently stir in the berries. Push the batter into the mold, cover tightly, place on a trivet in the pot and pour the hot water halfway up the sides of the mold. Cover the pot and maintain at a simmer for 1½ hours. Cool in the mold for five minutes, then turn the pudding out on a serving plate and serve at once, with Honey Butter, Honeyed Brandy Butter, or another sauce of your choice. Leftover pudding can be steamed in a double boiler; always serve hot with sauce. Another technique to refresh pudding is to slice and butter lightly, then fry until golden. Puddings will keep several days refrigerated; they also freeze well.

Toasted ALMOND PUMPKIN FLAN

½ cup sugar
½ cup blanched almonds, chopped
¼ cup hot water
1 cup unsweetened pumpkin puree
½ cup honey
½ tsp. salt
1½ cups evaporated milk
⅓ cup water
1 tsp. cinnamon
1½ tsp. vanilla
5 eggs

Preheat oven to 350°. Prepare a pan of hot water large enough to hold a 1½ quart baking dish (pie plate, pyrex dish, or souffle). Caramelize the sugar in a dry skillet over medium heat, watching closely and stirring as needed. When it has turned a rich golden brown, add the water, stirring until smooth again. Cool slightly. Meanwhile toast the almonds, spread in a single layer in a pan, in the oven for 10 minutes, until light brown. Stir them into the caramel and pour this mixture into the baking dish, tilting to line evenly. Mix together the pumpkin puree, honey, milk, and water, salt and flavorings. Beat the eggs and mix in thoroughly. Pour into the lined baking dish and set in the pan of hot water. Bake one hour and 10 minutes, or until only the center jiggles when pan is gently shaken. Cool, then refrigerate. Serve chilled and unmold to serve. Makes 8 servings.

SWEET-POTATO PONE

Sweet potato pone is at its best on a buffet with the South's finest: a Smithfield ham, scalloped potatoes, and beaten biscuits. It can be served as a dessert, plain or with Honey-Lemon Sauce, but this is not traditional.

¼ cup butter
⅓ cup brown sugar
⅓ cup honey
2 eggs
1 cup light cream
¾ tsp. salt
¾ tsp. nutmeg, freshly grated
2½ cups raw sweet potato, grated*
½ cup pecans, chopped

Preheat oven to 350°. Butter a 9″ pie plate or baking dish very heavily. Cream the butter and add sugar and honey; combine thoroughly. Beat in the eggs. Stir in cream and seasonings. Combine the grated sweet potato with the egg mixture; add nuts. Pour into the prepared pan and bake 50–60 minutes, until only the center jiggles when the pan is gently shaken. Serve hot, or warm; some people will even like it cold. Serves 8–10.

* A handheld Mouli grater can be used to grate potatoes; a Scandinavian nut grater is more convenient. Either way it takes some time to prepare this quantity. The potatoes can be peeled, cubed, placed in a blender jar to one half full and water added to half their depth. Blend on high speed a few minutes and they will be grated. Drain thoroughly in a strainer before adding to the batter.

HONEY ICE CREAM

This sensational ice cream is permeated with fresh orange flavor and studded with toasted almonds.

3 ½ cups heavy cream	1 tsp. almond extract
⅔ cup honey	¼ tsp. salt
grated rind of two oranges	⅔ cup almonds, toasted and chopped

Toast the almonds on a jelly roll pan in a 350° oven for 10 minutes or until golden. In a large mixing bowl, beat the cream until slightly thickened. Add the honey gradually, beating until the mixture is well blended. Stir in the orange rind, almond extract, and salt. Freeze in an ice cream maker, adding the nuts as the mixture begins to harden. Freeze until quite firm; then transfer to a bowl, covered container, or fancy mold, and let mellow in the freezer compartment for a few hours before serving. Makes about 2 quarts.

Greek MOLDED HONEY CHEESECAKE
Tyropeta

The antecedent of this Greek dish, introduced into Russia during the days of the Byzantine Empire, was translated into *pashka*, a molded cheese embellished with candied fruits that is still served in Russia at Easter.

1 ½ pounds ricotta cheese
2 Tbsp. honey
1 Tbsp. sweet white wine or cream sherry
¼ cup grated almonds

Combine the cheese, honey, and wine, beating until well blended. Butter a 1-quart mold, preferably a ring or some other decorative shape, and dust with some of the grated almonds. Add the rest to the cheese mixture, blending thoroughly. Press the cheese into the mold with your knuckles to pack it firmly and evenly. Smooth out any dents or depressions by running a rubber spatula across the cheese. Cover and chill 24 hours. To serve, dip the mold into hot water for three seconds, then invert on a serving plate. Surround with fresh strawberries, peaches, or apricots. Cut into wedges and serve with a portion of fruit.

HONEYED ORANGE CREAM, *English style*

This delicate concoction is derived from the orange fool served at a famous English men's club. Not oversweet, it is a perfect choice to follow a robust menu. In preparing the dessert, remember that the gelatin and whipped cream mixtures should be combined when they are similar in consistency; this avoids separating.

    1 Tbsp. unflavored gelatine
    ½ cup cold water
      grated rind of two oranges
      grated rind of one lemon
      the juice of four oranges
      the juice of two lemons
    2 Tbsp. honey, heather preferred
    1½ cups heavy cream

Dissolve gelatine in ½ cup cold water in a small bowl or metal measuring cup. Set in a small pan of simmering water and stir until clear. Grate the rinds of two oranges and one lemon directly into a large mixing bowl and add the fresh fruit juices. Stir in honey and the gelatine mixture.

Refrigerate until it begins to thicken and has the consistency of unbeaten egg whites. Whip the cream until it forms distinct mounds and gently fold the two mixtures together. Pour into a serving dish and chill overnight or at least four hours before serving. Garnish with rosettes of whipped cream, bits of candied orange peel, and mint leaves. 6 servings.

Armenian FRUITED WHEAT PUDDING
Anoush abour

Anoush abour is a favorite Armenian sweet associated with Christmas and other important occasions, such as the birth of a baby. Similar puddings are made in the Ukraine, where it is called *kutia*. A spoonful of *kutia* is tossed toward the ceiling; if it sticks, it is a sign that the bees will swarm and the next year's harvest will be bountiful.

1 cup whole wheat berries	10 dried apricots, cut in quarters
¼ tsp. salt, or as needed	2½ Tbsp. sugar
⅓ cup golden raisins	2½ Tbsp. honey
3 Tbsp. pine nuts	3 drops rose water
3 Tbsp. walnuts, chopped	cinnamon sugar, for garnish
3 Tbsp. blanched almonds, halved	chopped almonds or pistachios, for garnish

Wash the wheat with boiling water and drain. Place in a heavy saucepan with water to cover and bring to a boil. Boil two minutes, then cover and set aside for one hour. Or soak the grain overnight, then wash it and cook as above; these steps reduce the total cooking time. Drain the soaked wheat, return to the saucepan, add 2¾ cups boiling water, cover, and simmer very slowly until the grain is tender, four hours or more. Check once or twice to see if more boiling water is needed. When the grain is nearly tender, add salt cautiously, stirring in just enough to eliminate the bland, watery taste. The grain is done when it resembles a thick porridge, having absorbed the water during cooking. Add raisins, pine nuts, walnuts, almonds, apricots, sugar, honey, and rose water. Stir over low heat to dissolve the sugar, mixing thoroughly. Spoon into a serving bowl. Chill thoroughly. Serve with cinnamon sugar and chopped nuts. 8 generous servings.

Some versions of this recipe include no fruit; others use currants and dates in addition; some include poppyseed; still others are made with rice, not wheat. For more tang, add more apricots; for more sweetness, increase honey. Whole wheat berries are available at natural food and health food stores.

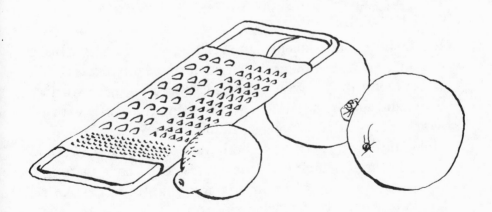

HAZELNUT HONEY CHARLOTTE
Charlotte au miel

Travel in France offers a special challenge when you consider the food as important as the landmarks. Routing must be meticulously planned so that you reach the chosen restaurant with an appetite to match the anticipated meal. One year we contemplated with joy dinner in Avignon at a one-star restaurant (the Michelin guide's mark for unpretentious, carefully prepared food) which promised *charlotte au miel*. The wonderful honey of Provence seldom appears on menus; it would be a treat. The restaurant was closed, we dined well elsewhere, and it was left for me to work out a formula for this charlotte.

1 Tbsp. unflavored gelatine	1 cup heavy cream, whipped
2 Tbsp. cold water	½ cup toasted hazelnuts, blanched and grated*
4 egg yolks	12–15 ladyfingers, homemade preferred
¼ cup sugar	
¼ cup honey	
1 cup milk, heated to the boil with 1″ vanilla bean	

In a small container dissolve the gelatine in cold water; place in a small pan of hot water and warm until the mixture is clear and smooth. Beat together the egg yolks and sugar; stir in honey and add the hot milk slowly, stirring constantly with a wire whip. Heat gently in a small, heavy saucepan, whisking often, until thickened and smooth. Remove the vanilla bean. Add the gelatine mixture and set aside to cool, stirring occasionally to prevent a skin from forming. Line a 1½ quart charlotte mold with ladyfingers, trimming those for the bottom to meet in the center in an attractive design. Use trimmings to fill in any unmatched corners. When the custard is cool but not firm, fold in the whipped cream and the hazelnuts. Pour into the prepared mold. Refrigerate until firm, several hours or overnight. Unmold and cut in wedges to serve.

* To prepare hazelnuts: Place in an open pan one layer deep in a 350° oven for 15 minutes, until they are fragrant. Remove and rub the nuts together in a towel; the brown skins will fall off. This can be difficult when the nuts are not fresh; they need not be perfectly blanched. The nuts should be toasted pale gold; if not, return to the oven a little longer. Cool and grate in a Swedish nut grinder or Mouli grater.

Middle Eastern ORANGE PUDDING
Flamri de semoule

People of many countries mix cereals and fruits in sweet combinations that are served, cold and hot, for dessert or snacks. This practice has not been popular with Americans; one reads occasionally of Appalachian "white mountain" (farina) puddings, but always as a dish of the past. Therefore this delicate molded orange pudding, probably Algerian in origin, has the taste of an exotic dessert far more than its simple ingredients would suggest.

½ cup orange juice	2 Tbsp. lemon juice
½ cup water	2 Tbsp. dry sherry
3 Tbsp. farina (Cream of Wheat cereal)	or 1 Tbsp. Cointreau
	rind of half an orange
3 Tbsp. honey	2 egg whites

Bring the orange juice and water to a boil in a small, heavy saucepan; sprinkle in the farina and cook until tender, stirring often, about 15 minutes. Remove from the heat and stir in honey, lemon juice, and liquor. Grate the orange rind directly into the pan. Cool. In a separate small dry bowl, beat the egg whites until they hold stiff peaks. Fold into the pudding while it is still soft. Chill in a bowl or simple mold, lightly oiled. Unmold and serve cold. 4 servings.

ARAB HONEY SWEET *Ekmek kadaif*

The ultimate honey sweet—bread soaked in warm honey syrup and served with cream thick enough to cut. The cream, unfortunately, is not readily available outside the Middle East, where it is obtained by boiling buffalo milk. I have had a delicious facsimile at an Armenian restaurant in New York, where I was told it was prepared by repeated pourings of warm cream from a distance of four feet into a basin; Indian friends from Delhi have described a cream dessert they make with eight hours' nurturing and pouring. Several writers suggest a less arduous method, combining a quart of milk with a cup of heavy cream and maintaining it at a barely wavering simmer for 1½ hours followed by 7 hours at room temperature and overnight refrigeration. The resulting layer of cream may be cut into squares. Whipped cream or homemade sour cream are also good accompaniments. The pastry is incredibly sweet and especially delicious, well worth planning a suitable menu to be followed by a morsel and cups of strong tea.

2 cups sugar	½ cup honey
1 cup water	one round loaf stale
the juice of half	bread, an inch thick
a lemon	and trimmed of crusts

Choose a heavy saucepan large enough to accommodate a round of stale bread trimmed from a round French or Italian loaf so that it is free of crusts and about an inch thick. In the saucepan, make a heavy syrup using the water, sugar, and lemon juice. Stir over medium heat until the sugar melts, then boil until it thickens. Stir in ½ cup honey; Greek hymettus honey is preferred. This recipe truly expresses the flavor of whatever honey is chosen. With the sauce at a simmer, immerse the bread. Turn it and push it into the syrup to help it absorb as much as possible. Twenty or thirty minutes, some of it unattended, can be allowed for this process. Remove the bread to a serving plate, basting with a little syrup. Cool and serve with cream.

CANDIED FRUIT PEELS *for baking*

Remove the peel from oranges or lemons in wide wedges, including the white pith but none of the fruit pulp. Blanch the peel in a large kettle of boiling water for 5 minutes; drain and repeat with fresh water up to five blanchings, as time permits. Drain and cool. Trim the soft rind into uniform ¼″ strips. Prepare a simple syrup in a large, heavy saucepan with 2 cups of water and 2 cups sugar. Stir over medium heat until the sugar is dissolved, then simmer about 10 minutes until it thickens. Drop the rind into the hot syrup and cook, partially covered, until translucent and impregnated with syrup, about 40 minutes. Cool in syrup. Cover a large surface, like a jelly-roll pan, with a light coating of granulated sugar; a sieve helps for even distribution. When the peel is cool, lift from the syrup, draining off any excess, and place in a single layer in the pan. Let dry uncovered overnight. Then place in an airtight container for storage. These keep a few weeks; freeze for longer storage. To make fruit peel confections with longer shelf life, scrape the white pulp from the peel after blanching and proceed as directed. These thin strips make refreshing candy.

I find that the rinds of four oranges and two lemons will fit a 10x15 baking pan, so I often make this quantity; I blanch the two together, although purists may wish to follow the one fruit–one pot rule. I save any leftover syrup in the refrigerator and add sugar and water in equal parts to make the volume needed for another batch. Pineapple may also be candied this way for baking; do not combine with other fruit in blanching or finishing. Cut the pineapple in large wedges or bite-size pieces.

GREEN GRAPES *with* PORT & HONEY

- 1 pound seedless green grapes
- 1 tsp. lemon juice
- 2 Tbsp. port
- ¼ cup honey

Wash and stem the grapes. Stir the lemon juice, port, and honey together in a non-metal bowl that can be covered easily. Mix in the grapes, cover, and refrigerate overnight. Serve in dessert dishes, spooning juices over the grapes. Some people may like this with sour cream, especially if they have a supply of home-soured cream. I prefer it plain, with a crisp cookie.

HOT HONEYED GRAPEFRUIT

For each serving:

> one half grapefruit
> 1 tsp. honey
> 1 Tbsp. sherry
> dash nutmeg, freshly grated
> cherry or a bit of ginger, for decoration

Preheat oven to 400°. Cut the grapefruit stem to stem and remove the segments, cutting out white membrane and re-assembling the fruit. Drizzle honey and sherry over the portions and grate a little nutmeg on top. Bake for 10 minutes, or until heated through. Garnish with a maraschino cherry or slice of preserved ginger and serve at once, either as a first course or dessert.

BROILED PINEAPPLE

1 fresh pineapple, pared, cored, and cut into chunks
     OR 1 large can unsweetened pineapple, well drained
honey to taste

Preheat broiler. Spread the pineapple chunks in an even layer in a broiler-proof serving dish. Drizzle lightly and evenly with honey. Broil 6 inches from heat for about 10 minutes, until bubbling and slightly browned at the edges. Spoon into dessert cups to serve hot.

HONEYDEW GINGER

An exceedingly simple and refreshing dessert or brunch dish is made by mixing together a tablespoon of honey and a teaspoon of ground ginger. Drizzle over wedges of honeydew melon.

SUMMER COMPOTE

4 large peaches	1 Tbsp. Grand Marnier
½ cup blueberries	or Curaçao
1 tsp. lemon juice	1½ Tbsp. honey
3 Tbsp. orange juice	

Scald the peaches to loosen their skins; peel and cut in thick slices. Place in a serving bowl and sprinkle with the lemon juice, to prevent discoloration. Add the blueberries. Combine the orange juice, liqueur, and honey and pour over the fruit, mixing gently. Cover and marinate in the refrigerator at least an hour. Accompany with a platter of honey cookies. Vary the fruits as they come in season.

FRUIT SALAD *with* HONEY & WINE

¾ cup white wine	2 ripe peaches
3 Tbsp. honey	3 ripe apricots
3 Tbsp. nuts, chopped	1 cup strawberries,
1 apple	or 3 or 4 ripe plums
1 ripe pear	

Mix wine and honey together; stir in nuts. Cut fruits in thin slices, peeling and trimming as needed. Combine in a serving bowl, coat gently with the dressing, and chill several hours before serving. Many combinations of fruit are delicious, but avoid using citrus fruits here.

PLUM SALAD, SOUR CREAM & HONEY

ripe fresh plums, four varieties if possible
sour cream
honey

Highly seasonal, this salad is a delicious celebration of the days of high summer when there are plums of many colors in the markets. Choose several distinctly different kinds—sweet yellow ones, firm dark red plums, prune plums with yellow, slightly mealy, interiors; cut them into quarters with as little violence as possible around the pits. Arrange in a serving dish and distribute sour cream generously around the bowl. Drizzle honey liberally over the arrangement. Accompanied by a simple fragrant bread, this will make a complete small meal; it is excellent after soup or a sandwich.

FRUIT WHIP

1 large peach or nectarine, peeled and cut up (about 1 cup)
1 cup yogurt
1 Tbsp. lemon juice
2 Tbsp. honey
nutmeg, freshly grated

Combine all ingredients in a blender jar and whirl until smooth. Chill or not, as desired. Pour into a tall glass to serve, and sprinkle with freshly grated nutmeg. This thick drink or light snack is subject to endless variations.

BASIC HONEY SYRUP *for pastries*

Mediterranean baked sweets are often soaked in honey syrup while still warm, then allowed to cool before serving. Straight honey would be too sweet and viscous for this and is usually diluted in a thin sugar syrup flavored with citrus and spices. Since honey syrup keeps well at room temperature, it can be made in large batches for storing in the pantry. This recipe gives proportions for one pound of honey. Thyme honey from Mt. Hymettus, available at Greek delicatessens and groceries, is the preferred flavor.

1 pound Hymettus honey	3 cinnamon sticks
2⅔ cups sugar	5 Tbsp. fresh lemon juice
2 cups water	2½ Tbsp. brandy
rind of one small lemon	

Combine the sugar, water, lemon rind in strips, cloves, and cinnamon in a saucepan and bring to a boil. Reduce heat and simmer until the syrup thickens slightly, 10 to 15 minutes. Strain out the rind and spices. Stir in the honey, lemon juice, and brandy. Cool; store in clean jars and use as needed for Greek pastries.

HONEYED BRANDY BUTTER

½ cup sweet butter
½ cup honey
2 Tbsp. brandy or rum
freshly-grated nutmeg

Cream the butter. Add the honey and blend thoroughly. Then add the brandy, a few drops at a time, beating until the mixture is fluffy. Add nutmeg to taste, transfer to a crock or small bowl, and chill thoroughly. Serve on steamed cranberry or blueberry pudding.

HONEY BUTTER

½ cup butter
¼ cup honey

Cream the butter, add honey and whip until fluffy and smooth. Store in small covered crocks, refrigerated, up to a week. This simple spread is wonderful on toast, pancakes, waffles, biscuits, cornbread, or warm gingerbread.

VARIATIONS: Add the grated rind of half an orange; blend well. OR Add 1 Tbsp. finely chopped toasted almonds. OR Add ¼ tsp. cinnamon.

WAFFLE SYRUP CURAÇAO

1 cup heavy cream
1 cup honey
¼ cup butter
2 Tbsp. Curaçao, Grand Marnier, or Triple Sec

In a saucepan combine the cream, honey, and butter and cook over medium heat 10 minutes, or until smooth and slightly thickened. Stir in Curaçao and cook a minute longer. Serve warm in a pitcher, with waffles or dishes of ice cream.

HONEY LEMON SAUCE

1 cup water
1 Tbsp. potato starch flour
½ cup honey (or less, to taste)
one lemon, rind and juice
1 Tbsp. butter

Dissolve the potato starch flour in the cold water. Place in a small saucepan and stir in the honey. Cook slowly until thickened and clear. Off the heat, grate the lemon rind directly into the pan so no aromatic oils are lost, then squeeze the lemon and strain juice into the sauce. Stir in butter. Serve warm with gingerbread, hot puddings, or apple pie.

SPICED HONEYED CREAM

1 cup cream
2 Tbsp. honey
½ tsp. cinnamon or other spices

Whip the cream until lightly thickened. Beat in the honey and cinnamon. Serve as a topping with pumpkin pie, fruit pies, and gingerbread.

Recommended Equipment

HEAVY-DUTY MIXER

A heavy-duty mixer makes short work of all whipping, creaming, kneading, and blending jobs. Equipped with wire whips, dough hooks, and mixing paddles, and with more powerful motors than found in other readily available mixers, these machines are a boon to the serious cook.

WIRE WHIPS

In lieu of a heavy-duty mixer, use wire whips to blend batters, mix sauces, and beat egg whites. Many shapes and sizes are available, in different gauges of steel, different degrees of flexibility. The stiff heavy-gauge variety is fine for beating and blending medium batters, but for whipping egg whites use a professional-quality whip of fine-guage steel with great flexibility. The more bounce in the whip, the faster air is beaten into the whites. Always choose stainless steel because tin-washed steel will rust. The tiniest whip available is perfect for blending salad dressings and marinades.

THERMOMETERS

In candy-making, frying, or baking, accurate temperature measurement is crucial. The final product will be dramatically different if the syrup boils too long, if the oil is not hot enough, or if the oven is actually 50 degrees cooler than the temperature indicated.

A candy thermomenter eliminates the need for judgmental sugar syrup tests ("cook until a bit of syrup forms a soft ball in cold water") and thus reduces the chance of failure due to under- or over-boiling of syrups and candies. A useful common style has a temperature range of from 100° F. to 314° F. and consists of a mercury column attached to a slender metal frame. Its advantage over the rod-and-dial type is that it needs not be so deeply immersed to give accurate readings.

The rod-and-dial type is really a two-in-one thermometer for both deep-fat frying and candy-making. It registers temperatures up to 400° F. Unless one has a great deal of experience in deep-fat frying, guessing oil temperatures is risky and wasteful. It is almost impossible to *maintain* an even oil temperature without a thermometer.

Ovens, especially old ones, are notoriously inaccurate and cause many disappointments and failures in otherwise perfectly prepared dishes. Therefore it is well worth your while to invest in an oven thermomenter and use it to calibrate your oven.

ROLLING PINS

A rolling pin must be heavy, preferably of solid hardwood such as maple, so that the weight of the pin itself does much of the work. Lightweight toy-like models available in supermarkets and most housewares departments are virtually useless. We recommend either the American ball-bearing variety or the heavy French boxwood cylinder.

COOLING RACKS

Wire cooling racks are absolutely essential for the proper "finishing" of baked goods. Air must be allowed to circulate all around a cooling cake or cookies to prevent the bottoms from becoming soggy and steamy. Two 10x14 wire racks will accommodate most baking operations.

ELECTRIC SPICE GRINDER

Freshly ground spices have an incomparable fragrance and potency. A small electric coffee mill is excellent for grinding small quantities of spices such as cinnamon, allspice, cloves, ginger. It is easy to fill, does the job quickly, and is easy to clean out between batches.

MORTAR AND PESTLE

A small mortar and pestle of wood, glass porcelain, or marble is useful in crushing cardamon, anise, or fennel seeds, and is generally handy for grinding herbs and spices.

NUTMEG GRATER

Unchanged in style for generations, the nutmeg grater is beautiful, inexpensive, and a pleasure to use. Keep one on a peg near your spice rack, with a whole nutmeg stored inside.

SWEDISH NUT GRINDER

This is a small metal grater with a rotating drum, which clamps onto a table or counter edge and makes quick work of nut grinding. It is easier to use than hand-held rotary models for grating carrots or sweet potatoes.

CITRUS GRATER

Specialty cooking equipment shops carry the small flat graters designed specifically for grating the peel from lemons, oranges, and limes, but the finest grate of a larger, general-purpose flat grater will also do the job nicely and may in fact be easier to hold over a mixing bowl for grating fresh citrus rind directly into a batter.

RUBBER SPATULAS

These familiar gadgets come in at least two sizes, the narrower version being just right for scraping honey from a small jar or measuring cup. The larger size is excellent for folding beaten egg whites into batters and for scraping bowls clean.

DOUGH SCRAPER

A wide, flat metal blade with a wood handle running the length of one side, used for scraping sticky dough from the pastry board as you knead. It is also handy for lifting and transferring chopped ingredients from board to bowl and for leveling cups of sugar or flour as they are measured.

PASTRY BRUSH

Needed for painting glazes on breads, brushing melted butter on pastries, basting meats, and greasing pans. The natural bristle, paint-brush style is most durable and efficient.

PASTRY BLENDER

Used for cutting butter or shortening into flour, the first step in making pie crust.

HONEY DISPENSER

A German gadget that allows one to transfer honey from crock to toast without dripping on the table. It consists of a plastic wand with a beehive-shaped knob on the end. The knob picks up and holds a ball of honey without dripping, as long as one rotates the wand slowly. When the wand is held steady the honey drips, but it can be turned off simply by rotating the wand again. Very handy for measuring small quantities of honey.

TWO-CUP MEASURING CUP

Useful when a recipe asks you to combine several ingredients before adding them to the rest of the batter.

CAKE TESTER

More hygienic than a broom straw, this slender piece of wire is long enough to test the deepest breads. A trace of moisture indicates that a little more baking is needed.

Basic pan sizes

Loaf pans ᐧᐧ 9x5: For breads and cakes, the standard size. 2 quart capacity, it is usually metal. 8x4: For breads and cakes, 1½ quart capacity. Usually glass; bake at 25° lower oven heat. Small foil pans: Three of these disposable pans hold the equivalent of a 9x5 pan. While they do not brown as evenly as a heavier pan, they make a convenient size for gift-giving.

Baking sheets ᐧᐧ For cookies, breads, and pastries. Available in different dimensions; convenient to have two or more. Choose the largest and heaviest available. A 10x15 jelly roll pan may be used, with the slight disadvantage that its low sides may interfere with removing the baked goods.

Pie plate ᐧᐧ For pies and breads. Standard size is 9″. Ceramic ones conduct heat best, producing flaky brown crust. Pyrex lets you judge the doneness of the crust. Foil pans are least desirable.

Rectangular baking pans ᐧᐧ 9x13 is a standard size, with deep sides for making large cakes and coffeecakes; generally metal. Smaller pyrex rectangles are available but recipes must be scaled down to fit; bake at 25° lower oven heat.

Square baking pans ᐧᐧ Both 9x9 and 8x8 are frequently called for. Available in metal or glass. One half of a recipe for a 9x9 pan can be baked in a 9x5 loaf pan.

French tart tins ᐧᐧ For sweet tarts or quiche, these are shallow pans with a fluted edge and removable bottom. 9″ size yields 8 servings, 8″ 6 servings. A full recipe for a 9″ pie can be made in two 9″ tart pans. The rings are removed when the pastries are hot, permitting good circulation in cooling.

Foil pie plates ⌒ For bread. Shallow foil pie plates are convenient for shaping round loaves: the sides provide just enough support to create handsome loaves. Fill with flattened balls of dough not quite large enough to cover the flat bottom of the pan, and they will rise in proper proportion.

The authors, Gene Opton and Nancie Hughes, feel that few activities give more pleasure than sharing good food with friends. Appreciating the natural tastes and textures of foods is basic to good cooking and eating. Call it a respect for ingredients: a good cook not only insists on the freshest and best but takes the time to prepare them well. And a happy guest knows that he is cared for when he is offered lovingly prepared and appealingly presented food — whether it is simple fare or a feast.

In 1967 Gene established a store, The Kitchen, as a source of fine cooking equipment and information for the Berkeley community; she also has been manager (and sometimes cook) at a French restaurant in Berkeley. Nancie has worked at The Kitchen since 1969. Georgianna Greenwood, designer of Honey Feast, has long designed printed materials for the shop.